John!
Never stop believing!

AERIAL
PHENOMENA

REVIVING UFOLOGY FOR THE 21ST CENTURY

By Antonio Paris

Aerial Phenomena

Copyright © 2012 by Antonio Paris

www.aerial-phenomenon.org

All rights reserved. Without limiting the rights under copyright reserved above, no part of this publication may be reproduced, stored in or introduced into a retrieval system, or transmitted, in any form, or by any means (electronic, mechanical, photocopying, recording, or otherwise) without the prior written permission of the copyright owner of this book.

ISBN 978-1-4675-4927-1

United States Copyright Office

November 2012

Published and printed in the United States of America

This book is dedicated to my sister Jessica.

Nothing ever truly dies; the universe wastes nothing.

Facts are stubborn things; and whatever may be our wishes, our inclinations, or the dictates of our passions, they cannot alter the state of facts and evidence.

-- John Adams, 1770

TABLE OF CONTENTS

Acknowledgments 7

Note from the Author 9

Introduction 10

Chapter One: The UFO Investigative Process 14

Chapter Two: The Case Files 27

Chapter Three: The Analysis 130

Chapter Four: Reviving Ufology 136

Glossary 143

References 148

Your Notes 151

ACKNOWLEDGEMENTS

The Aerial Phenomenon Investigations Team (API) is comprised of a former special agent, an intelligence analyst, a spacecraft engineer, senior-level educators, scientists, and other professionals dedicated to investigating, researching, and analyzing Unidentified Flying Objects (UFOs) and other alleged extraterrestrial encounters. The UFO phenomena, specifically extraterrestrial abductions, are challenging to investigate; these investigations cannot be conducted strictly behind a computer. Regarding the UFO and alleged extraterrestrial encounter cases discussed in this book, API spent over 2,000 hours adhering to a well-proven investigative process to draw its investigative conclusions. Throughout the investigations in this book, API:

- Interviewed witnesses, officials, and experts, including law enforcement officials and

members of federal agencies, academia, and the defense industry.
- Conducted field forensics at locations of alleged UFO activity.
- Worked in a lab environment to analyze alleged physical evidence of extraterrestrial objects.
- Analyzed hours of video footage and hundreds of photos of alleged extraterrestrial spacecraft or entities.
- Conducted investigative research and analysis on topics such as astronomy, aeronautics, meteorology, and UFO phenomena, among others.

I am proud of my team for their hard work and dedication to a complex issue. An immense appreciation and thank you, therefore, is warranted to the following:

- **Paul Carr:** Deputy Director and Chief Scientist
- **Cherish Holt:** Photographer and Video Technician
- **Marsha Barnhart:** Senior Field Investigator
- **Charles Fonner:** Senior Field Investigator
- **Ken Pfeifer:** Senior Field Investigator
- **Shane Sovar:** International Field Investigator
- **Craig Newton:** Field Investigator and Media Relations
- **Ray Nuvolone:** Abductee Field Investigator
- **Pat Colbert:** Field Investigator
- **Nancy Doty:** Field Investigator
- **Jacqueline Jackson:** Field Investigator
- **Pat Ciuffreda:** UFO Research Analyst

NOTE FROM THE AUTHOR

This book is not intended to debate whether or not extraterrestrial life exists, or for that matter, what any extraterrestrial's agenda might be. Likewise, this book is not meant to entertain the physics of interstellar travel, inter-dimensional beings, alleged top secret anti-gravity propulsion systems, or conspiracy theories regarding alleged U.S. government efforts to reverse-engineer extraterrestrial technology. In its strictest sense, this book removes the extraterrestrial element from the equation, approaches UFO investigations from a nuts-and-bolts perspective, and analyzes *known data*, not speculation, in an effort to make sense of the phenomena. This effort, I hope, will educate the reader about UFOs and, more importantly, demonstrate that evidence of extraterrestrial visitation is lackluster at best.

INTRODUCTION

An unidentified flying object (UFO), in its strictest sense, is an unfamiliar anomaly in the sky that is not readily identifiable to the observer as any known object.[1] Technically, "UFO" refers to something that cannot be identified; unfortunately, in contemporary popular culture, the term has become synonymous with extraterrestrial spacecraft. However, decades of investigations, research, and analysis from a cadre of UFO investigators, including the United States Air Force, have established that most UFO sightings are either hoaxes or misidentifications of man-made terrestrial objects and natural phenomena.[2] Evidence of extraterrestrial life remains elusive as ever.

The lack of physical and scientific proof beyond a reasonable doubt has pushed UFOs to be regarded along with Bigfoot, the Loch Ness Monster, the chupacabra, and leprechauns: subjects nestled together in the occult section of your local bookstore or library. This unfortunate occurrence, in my opinion, is a direct result of a once-worthy subject being hijacked by a convergence of armchair UFO investigators, conspiracy theorists, hoaxers, and people taking occasional cheesy photos of alleged extraterrestrials or flying saucers.

In early 2011, in an effort to revive and revolutionize Ufology, I decided to investigative UFO phenomena for myself. First, to clean up Ufology, I needed to remove the extraterrestrial element from the equation and approach the phenomena from a nuts-and-bolts perspective. Second, I needed to find or create a well-proven investigative process to make sense of the data. Therefore, I developed the Aerial Phenomena Investigations Guide comprised of the knowledge I gained in graduate school (in space studies and planetary science) and the investigative skills I acquired as an Army counterintelligence officer and a special agent for the Department of Defense Counterintelligence Field Activity.[3] With my new vision regarding Ufology, I went on to create a new UFO research group made up of like-minded professionals. My vision, which I knew would get initial pushback from mainstream Ufologists, was to recruit UFO enthusiasts willing to respectively set aside the extraterrestrial hypothesis and approach the phenomena from a "detective's perspective".

In the middle of 2011, I began to attend dozens of UFO-related meetings and conferences throughout the United States, specifically in the Maryland, Virginia, and Washington, D.C., areas. As I expected, the premise behind most, if not all, of these UFO meetings and conferences were centered around the following:

- Conspiracies about the alleged Roswell UFO crash.
- Secret "world government" efforts to hide proof of extraterrestrial evidence from the public.
- Occasional hearsay of a deathbed confession from a retired military or intelligence official claiming first-hand knowledge of extraterrestrials.
- Setting aside all known laws of physics to argue for inter-dimensional portals that allow beings from other parts of the universe to travel to our planet at free will.

At none of these UFO meetings or conferences, however, could people provide proof, beyond a reasonable doubt, to substantiate these claims. In the end, I came to realize most, if not all, of these stories were just folklore with an added touch of hysteria and pareidolia (see glossary).

Nearly one year later, on December 3, 2011, I held my first Ufology meeting in Annapolis, MD. There, I presented my own perspective on UFO phenomena and recruited like-minded individuals to a new UFO research team. Setting aside the occasional sidebar regarding little green (or gray) men, the kickoff meeting was a success, and we founded the Aerial Phenomenon Investigations Team (API).

Aerial Phenomena field investigators conducting forensics and evidence collection training in 2012.

Today, our API mission is to conduct a systematic search for facts in order to determine whether or not a UFO sighting or alleged alien abduction can be attributed to a man-made object, natural phenomena, or a hoax. Our team accomplishes this by conducting aggressive investigative research and analysis; then, we assimilate, evaluate, and interpret a variety of reports on aerial phenomena. Throughout every investigation, we consider information derived from all credible sources and integrate it into our analytical process. API sets a high standard to obtain and provide proof, beyond a reasonable doubt, that a UFO or an alien abduction is of extraterrestrial origin. After a year of conducting dozens of thorough UFO investigations, we found no proof of extraterrestrial visitation. Nevertheless, the results of API's investigations do not mean that extraterrestrial life does not exist or, for that matter, that extraterrestrial life has not visited our planet. We identified most of the UFOs as terrestrial objects, closing very few cases in the "unidentified" file.

CHAPTER ONE

THE UFO INVESTIGATIVE PROCESS, DATA COLLECTION, AND TOOLS OF THE TRADE

We can't have full knowledge all at once. We must start by believing; then afterwards we may be led on to master the evidence for ourselves.

-- Thomas Aquinas, 1200s

THE INVESTIGATIVE PROCESS

In an effort to spare the reader a description of the countless hours spent on each UFO investigation, in Chapter Two I only provide a synopsis of the UFO cases my team investigated, along with the results of the investigations. I want to stress that these UFO investigations were not conducted willy-nilly. Instead, the team received, conducted and finalized the investigations using a well-proven investigative process that is part of a larger Case Management System (CMS).

By converging an array of investigative, space studies, and credible UFO manuals, I developed my Aerial Phenomena Investigations Guide, which has provided investigative guidance to API. The scope of the Aerial Phenomena Investigations Guide provides team members with the minimum tactics, techniques, and procedures (TTP) required to aggressively investigate whether or not a UFO can be attributed to a man-made object, natural phenomenon, or hoax. The guide stresses the duties and the importance of the Case Control Office, which exercises technical control, review, coordination, and oversight of all activities conducted by API.

Our intent with the API investigative process, which we sometimes refer to as the "investigative cycle," is to developed unrefined data from each UFO case into polished information used in writing the Report of Investigation (ROI). The investigative process, which consists of six steps, is circular in nature, although movement between the steps is fluid. For example, if an investigator uncovers certain information during a UFO investigation at one step, the new knowledge may require the investigator to go back to an earlier step before moving forward with the investigation. These six steps, in their simplest terms, are as follows:

- **Planning and Developing Direction:** When tasked with a specific case, the UFO investigator begins planning and establishing the scope of what he or she will do and how. The team, as a whole, conducts a case review meeting and discusses ways to gather the necessary data.

- **Collecting Data (See the separate section below on data collection):** The investigators collect information openly, which means they make no attempts to obtain classified national security information or conduct surreptitious surveillance of witnesses. Their data collection effort includes the following:

    o Conducting interviews with witnesses, officials, experts, and academics from a wide range of fields.
    o Making site visits to locations of alleged UFO activity.
    o Recording their findings through photography and videography.
    o Reading credible local newspaper and magazine articles that are not associated with conspiracies.
    o Listening to news on the radio and watching television news

broadcasts to obtain any relevant data concerning a UFO case.
  o Conducting open-source research on the Internet and at local libraries and museums.

- **Processing the Data:** The investigators fuse the information they have collected and shape it into the ROI. The information they provide in the ROI includes witness testimony and a detailed description of the UFO. The initial ROI is fluid, too, which means that at times the investigators will add or remove information as the UFO investigation evolves.

- **Analyzing the Information:** In this step, the investigators take a closer look at all the information they have gathered and determine how it fits together. The investigators assess what is happening, why it is happening, and what might occur next.

- **Finalizing the ROI:** Once the investigators have completed it, the final ROI documents the investigation's results. The final ROI includes a synopsis of the initial report; information developed during data collection, data processing, and analysis; and the investigation results. The team then closes all investigations under the heading of either "object identified" or "object unidentified."

- **Case Disposition:** When they have completed the ROI, the team provides a copy to the witness or witnesses. If appropriate, the team takes witness feedback, conducts a follow-up interview, and incorporates the additional information into the ROI. When the case is closed, the team archives the ROI in the Case Management System.

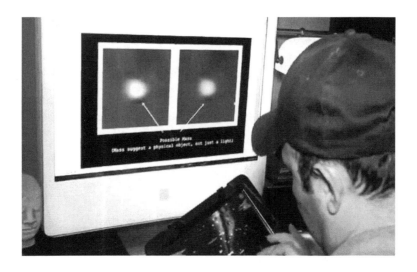

API Photo: The application of advanced analytics is an instrumental part of the investigative process.

DATA COLLECTION

Through these investigations, the team has found that the causes of the majority of UFO reports can be explained as sightings of man-made objects and natural phenomena, hoaxes, or even hallucinations. When people submit UFO reports to API, the assigned lead investigator conducts a preliminary assessment to determine whether there is a plausible explanation for what the witness saw. If the investigator cannot determine the nature of the object through a preliminary assessment, the team then opens the investigation as a Full-Field Investigation (FFI).

Using the least intrusive means possible, the investigators conduct indices checks on the witness or witnesses to confirm contact information and to determine whether or not any witnesses are associated with past hoaxes, conspiracy groups, and so forth. During the witness interview, the investigators use an extensive questionnaire to collect as much first-hand information regarding the UFO sighting as possible. At a minimum, the investigator is required to collect the following information:

- Location of sighting
- Date of sighting
- Time of sighting
- Rating scale (see next section)
- Case synopsis
- Duration of event
- Location of the witness

- Witness activity at the time of the event
- Nearest airport activity (commercial, military, and private)
- Nearest military base(s) activity
- Nearest space port activity
- Meteorology (date and time the event occurred):
  - Clouds
  - Winds
  - Precipitation
  - Temperature
  - Visibility
  - Astronomical data
- Data collection:
  - Shape of the UFO
  - Color of the UFO
  - Approximate size of the UFO from the witness's location
  - Actual size of the UFO (if known)
  - Direction of travel
  - Speed of the UFO (if known)
  - Answers to the following questions:
    - Did the UFO land?
    - Did the UFO change shape?
    - Any electronic disturbances?
    - Any occupants or pilots visible?
    - Any unusual maneuvers?
    - Any unusual markings?
    - Any heat from the UFO?
    - Any smoke or exhaust from the UFO?
    - Any lights or strobes from the UFO?
    - Any smell from the UFO?

- - Any noise from the UFO?
  - Any aircraft in the immediate area?
- Evidence collected from the witness:
  - Photos
  - Videos
  - Sketches
  - Voices
  - Physical material
  - Other
- Field site visit (search for physical traces):
  - Detection of radiation, if any
  - Detection of electromagnetic traces, if any
  - Detection of metal, if any
  - Documentation of on-site forensic photography
  - Other
- Investigator steps conducted:
  - Analysis of the MUFON Database (see glossary)
  - Analysis of the NUFORC Database (see glossary)
  - Analysis of the satellite orbital elements
  - Analysis of the photos or videos
  - Analysis of lens flares
  - Extraction of EXIF data (see glossary)
  - Assessment of terrain and area

Additionally, the Case Control Office assigns each of the investigated UFO cases a unique number including the following: the year the UFO case was opened, a number (in sequential order) indicating when the case was received, and the type of phenomena under investigation based on the Jacques Vallée UFO classification system.[4] This UFO classification system is composed of four different categories that are each divided into five subcategories:

1. **AN (Any anomalous phenomena):**

   - AN1: Anomalies that leave temporary physical effects, such as lights in the sky and similar phenomena.

   - AN2: Anomalies that leave lasting physical effects, such as crop circles, scorched earth, and debris.

   - AN3: Anomalies with associated occupants or entities.

   - AN4: Anomalies including interaction of a witness with occupants or entities.

   - AN5: Anomalous reports of injury, recovery, or death (for example, those involving unexplained wounds, healing of wounds, or spontaneous human combustion).

2. **MA Rating (Describes the UFO's maneuvering):**

   - MA1: A visual sighting of a UFO that travels in a discontinuous trajectory, which could mean making loops, quick turns, or vast changes in altitude.

- MA2: A visual sighting of a UFO that corresponds to physical evidence, such as burn marks or material fragments.

- MA3: A visual sighting of a UFO that has living entities on or around it.

- MA4: A visual sighting of UFO activity, such as maneuvers, accompanied by a change in the observer's perception of reality.

- MA5: A visual sighting of UFO activity that results in the witness's injury or death.

3. **FB Rating (Type of UFO fly-by):**

    - FB1: A fly-by of a UFO traveling in a straight line across the sky.

    - FB2: A fly-by of a UFO traveling in a straight line across the sky, leaving some kind of physical evidence.

    - FB3: A fly-by of a UFO traveling in a straight line across the sky, during which entities are observed.

    - FB4: A fly-by during which the witness experiences a sensation of unreality (e.g., a phantasmagoric state).

    - FB5: A fly-by that causes permanent injury to, or the death of, the witness.

4. **CE Rating (A close encounter):**

   - CE1: A visual sighting of a UFO within 500 feet.

   - CE2: A visual sighting of a UFO within 500 feet, which corresponds to physical evidence.

   - CE3: A visual sighting of a UFO that has entities aboard.

   - CE4: An encounter in which a witness experiences an abduction.

   - CE5: An encounter in which an abducted witness suffers physical or psychological injuries or death.

TOOLS OF THE TRADE

To assist their investigation, the team takes the API toolkit with them to a site where an alleged UFO sighting or alien abduction occurred. The toolkit contains the minimum recommended items outlined in many professional investigative manuals. Although API's toolkit is large and constantly growing, it includes the following at a minimum:

- Canon 60D-DSLR HD camera
- Canon EF 70-300 mm with a 4-5.6 IS USM telephoto lens
- Canon EF-S 18-135 mm with a 3.5-5.6 IS zoom lens
- Canon EF 28-80 mm with a 3.5-5.6 USM Lens
- AstroScope Generation III night vision lens for Canon 60D
- PVS7-3 Generation III night vision goggles
- 180 Zoom DV stereo microphone
- 850nM LED high power infrared illuminator pane
- RADALERT 100 radiation detector (detects Alpha-, Beta-, Gamma- and X-rays)
- Trifield Meter, model 100XE
- Pioneer 505 metal detector
- Rangefinder
- Basic investigations guide
- Compass
- GPS
- Magnifying glass

- Maps of the area
- Sketching paper
- Pencils
- Star charts (hardcopy and digital)
- Ziploc bags
- Tape measure and ruler
- Flashlight
- Latest weather report
- Tweezers
- Digital audio recorder
- Binoculars
- Supply of tent stakes
- Small garden trowel
- Small shovel
- Latex gloves
- 100 feet of line for setting up archeological site
- Computer laptop and tablet with an array of investigative and forensics software

CHAPTER TWO

**THE CASE FILES:
SYNOPSES OF 50 UFO INVESTIGATIONS**

*If it is a miracle, any sort of evidence will answer.
But if it is fact, proof is necessary.*

-- Mark Twain

CASE: 12-059-FB1

Location: Grimsby, U.K.

Date of Event: 12 June 2012

Description: UFO

Case Status: Identified

Findings: Artificial Satellite

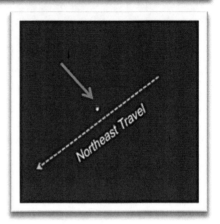

Synopsis: On 12 June 2012, at 22:13 hours, the witness to this sighting saw a UFO traveling northeast near Grimsby, U.K. The witness captured the UFO on a Forscam infrared webcam mounted on the roof of the witness's home.

Evidence Submitted: Video footage.

Initial Action: The team opened this UFO investigation as an FB1: a fly-by of a UFO traveling in a straight line across the sky. The team's preliminary analysis of the video indicated the UFO was, more than likely, an artificial satellite in Low Earth Orbit (LEO).

Investigation and Findings: The team performed indices checks on several satellite tracking databases, all of which indicated the UFO was space junk; more specifically, the UFO was the Cosmos 1953 Rocket in LEO. The Cosmos 1953 Rocket passed over the witness's location at the same date and time (22:13 hours on 12 June 2012) as reported by the witness. Additionally, the magnitude of the satellite was 2.4, which would have been visible on the webcam.

Object Details: The Cosmos 1953 Rocket[5] (*U.S. Space Command Catalog* No. 19210) was a Soviet ELINT (Electronic and Signals Intelligence) satellite launched from the Plesetsk Cosmodrome on 14 June 1988. The satellite remains in LEO with an apogee of 583 km and a perigee of 559 km (see glossary for the definition of apogee and perigee).

CASE: 12-050-AN1

Location: Washington, D.C.

Date of Event: 20 July 2012

Description: Alien Probe

Case Status: Identified

Findings: The Star Vega

Synopsis: At 22:00 hours on 20 July 2012, the witness to this sighting observed an extraterrestrial probe "zigzagging over the Washington, D.C., area." The witness believed the extraterrestrial probe was attempting to "disguise itself as a normal star" in an effort to conduct clandestine surveillance of the Washington, D.C., area.

Evidence Submitted: Video footage and still images from the video.

Initial Action: The team opened this UFO investigation as an AN1: an anomaly that left temporary physical effects, such as lights in the sky and similar phenomena. The team's preliminary analysis of the video indicated the UFO was, more than likely, a celestial object moving in and out of focus.

Investigation and Findings: On 29 July 2012, a team of investigators traveled to Washington, D.C., to interview the witness. According to the witness, the White House and the Search for Extra-Terrestrial Intelligence Institute (SETI) did not respond to the witness's UFO report, so he contacted API. During the interview, the investigators noticed the witness displayed signs of pareidolia and insisted that extraterrestrials were trying to "communicate a hidden message" to him. At the conclusion of the interview, the witness indicated the investigators should remain in the area because the extraterrestrial probe would appear at 21:00 hours.

At 21:15 hours, while waiting for the extraterrestrial probe to appear, the witness pointed to a star in the sky and said, "There is the extraterrestrial probe."

During the on-site investigation, the investigators concluded the object in the sky was the star Vega, not an extraterrestrial probe. The investigators were able to replicate the video the witness had provided by using a Canon 60D digital camera on autofocus and by holding the camera with one hand. After completing the experiment, the team's results were nearly identical to what the witness had submitted as evidence. The growing and shrinking appearance of the extraterrestrial probe was actually the camera's optics, which were attempting to focus on Vega. Additionally, the team identified the blue and red colors in the probe as natural phenomena (known as "atmospheric prismatic dispersion"); the zigzagging appearance of the probe was the result of the witness holding the camera with an unsteady hand.

Object Details: The star Vega is the fifth-brightest star visible from Earth and the third-brightest star easily visible from mid-northern latitudes. At about twenty-five light-years in distance, it is the sixth closest of all the bright stars, or fifth if you exclude Alpha Centauri, which is not easily visible from most of the Northern Hemisphere.⁶

CASE: 12-046-AN1

Location: Jakarta, Indonesia

Date of Event: 07 July 2012

Description: UFO

Case Status: Identified

Findings: Lens Flare

Synopsis: On 7 July 2012, at 14:00 hours, the witness to this sighting was taking photos of the sky with a mobile phone. While reviewing the photos, the witness noticed a strange object in one of them. The witness submitted the photo to API for analysis.

Evidence Submitted: A photo of a UFO.

Initial Action: The team opened this UFO investigation as an AN1: an anomaly that left temporary physical effects, such as lights in the sky and similar phenomena. The team's preliminary analysis of the video indicated the UFO was, more than likely, a catadioptric lens flare.

Investigation and Findings: During the interview, the witness claimed not to have personally observed the UFO when taking the photos of the sky, which is a common indicator of a lens flare. The team's analysis of the photo also indicated the sun was within the frame of view, a fact that indicated the likely source of the lens flare. In an effort to positively identify the object as a lens flare, the investigators obtained the original photo and applied standard cross-section analysis to it. Their analysis of the photo indicated the anomaly had intersected with the sun inside the frame of view, creating a lens flare.

Object Details: Lens flares are created when non-image-forming light enters the lens and subsequently hit the camera's film or digital sensor.[7] The lens flare often appears as a polygonal shape, giving the appearance of a "flying disk or saucer."

CASE: 12-057-FB1

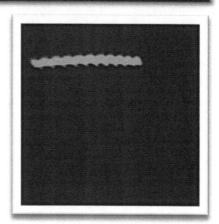

Location: Grimsby, U.K.

Date of Event: 10 June 2012

Description: UFO

Case Status: Identified

Findings: An Insect

Synopsis: On 10 June 2012, at 23:00 hours, the witness to this sighting used a webcam to capture a photo of "a strange UFO" in the vicinity of Grimsby, U.K. The witness captured the UFO on a Forscam infrared webcam mounted on the roof of the witness's home.

Evidence Submitted: Four photos of the UFO.

Initial Action: The team opened this UFO investigation as an FB1: a fly-by of a UFO traveling in a straight line across the sky. The team's preliminary analysis of the photo indicated the UFO was, more than likely, an insect.

Investigation and Findings: The team conducted indices checks on several UFO-related databases, including the Mutual UFO Network (MUFON) and the National UFO Reporting Center (NUFORC), which yielded no information relevant to this sighting. The team's additional research on several cryptozoology websites subsequently identified the unidentified object captured on the webcam as an insect. Moreover, the team discovered an array of additional photos of flying insects that matched the photo provided by the witness.

Object Details: In cryptozoology and outdoor photography, people often observe rods (sometimes known as "skyfish" or "solar entities"), which are elongated artifacts produced by cameras that inadvertently capture several wing-beats made by a flying insect.[8] Some people have claimed videos of rod-shaped objects moving quickly through the air are extraterrestrial life forms or small UFOs; however, subsequent experiments have shown that these rods appear in photos because of optical illusions.[9]

CASE: 12-055-MA4

Location: Richmond, VA

Date of Event: 06 Aug. 2012

Description: UFO

Case Status: Identified

Findings: Clouds

Synopsis: On 6 Aug. 2012, at 19:00 hours, the witness to this sighting was outside, on a balcony, and noticed a cloud shaped "like a flying saucer." The witness, who submitted several photos of these "cloudships," also reported that extraterrestrials were trying to warn the witness about "Earth's impeding doom."

Evidence Submitted: Twelve photos of various cloudship UFOs.

Initial Action: The team opened this UFO investigation as an MA4: UFO activity, such as maneuvers, accompanied by a change in the observer's perception of reality. The team's preliminary analysis of the photo indicated the UFO was, more than likely, a type of cloud.

Investigation and Findings: During the initial witness interview, the investigator noticed the witness displayed signs of pareidolia; the witness also insisted that extraterrestrials were "trying to hide their spaceships by camouflaging them as clouds." Several follow-up interviews further indicated the witness possessed the deep belief that an "extraterrestrial invasion was imminent." However, the team conducted an analysis of historical weather for the Richmond, VA, area specifically during the date and time the photo was taken, which indicated the weather was overcast with occasional showers. It is more than likely, therefore, that the witness took a photo of a cumulus humilis cloud.

Object Details: The cumulus humilis cloud is a low altitude cloud that can take many shapes and forms. These types of clouds indicate instability in the layering of air given appropriate convection or turbulence.[10]

CASE: 12-052-FB1

Location: Huntington, MD

Date of Event: 04 June 2012

Description: UFO

Disposition: Identified

Findings: Artificial Satellite

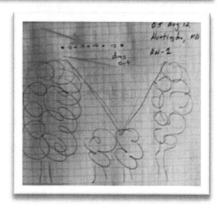

Synopsis: On 4 June 2012, at 22:37 hours, the witness to this sighting observed "a star-like object moving in the night." The object traveled across the sky from north to south for approximately three to ten seconds before disappearing. The witness also reported the object had about the same brightness as that of a star and made no noise or unusual maneuvers.

Evidence Submitted: A sketch of the UFO.

Initial Action: The team opened this UFO case as an FB1: a fly-by of a UFO traveling in a straight line across the sky. The team's preliminary analysis of the UFO description and sketch indicated the UFO was, more than likely, a man-made satellite in LEO.

Investigation and Findings: On 5 Aug. 2012, a team of investigators traveled to Huntington, MD, and interviewed the witness to this UFO sighting. The witness described the UFO as a star-like object that traveled from north to south until it disappeared over the horizon. The witness also pointed to the area in the sky where she observed the object, which the team calculated as appearing at 42° above the horizon. After the interview, investigators conducted indices checks on satellite tracking databases and identified the UFO as space junk; more specifically, they determined it was the Cosmos 1733 Rocket in LEO. The Cosmos 1733 Rocket passed over the witness's location on the same date the witness observed the UFO (4 June 2012) and at the same time (22:38 hours). Moreover, the Cosmos 1733 was traveling in the same direction (north to south) as that reported by the witness.

Object Details: The Cosmos 1733 Rocket[11] (*U.S. Space Command Catalog* No. 16611) was a Soviet ELINT satellite launched from the Plesetsk Cosmodrome on 20 Feb. 1986. The satellite remains in LEO with an apogee of 552 km and a perigee of 539 km.

CASE: 12-012-AN1

Location: Waldorf, MD

Date of Event: 15 July 2011

Description: UFO

Disposition: Identified

Findings: Specular Reflection

Synopsis: On 15 July 2011, at approximately 17:30 hours, the witness to this UFO investigation was traveling home from work. While at a stoplight, the witness used a cell phone to take a photo of a rainbow across the horizon. While reviewing the photos, the witness noticed two red orbs "in front of the rainbow."

Evidence Submitted: A photo of the UFO.

Initial Action: The team opened this UFO investigation as an AN1: an anomaly that left temporary physical effects, such as lights in the sky and similar phenomena. The team's preliminary analysis of the photo indicated the UFO was, more than likely, a reflection of the car's interior dashboard lights.

Investigation and Findings: During an interview, the witness indicated he had taken the photo inside the vehicle with the windows raised. Moreover, the witness did not notice the two red orbs prior to taking the photo, which indicated that the objects were likely reflections. After numerous attempts, the investigators were able to replicate the event and reproduce the orbs. Therefore, in an instance of specular reflection, the two red orbs reflected the dashboard lights inside the car.

Object Details: Specular reflection is the mirror-like reflection of light from a surface in which light from a single, incoming direction is reflected onto a single, outgoing direction[12]; in this case, the instrument lights from the dashboard reflected off the glass window.

CASE: 12-029-AN1

Location: Marseille, France

Date of Event: 21 Apr. 2012

Description: UFO

Disposition: Identified

Findings: Image Artifacts

Synopsis: On 21 Apr. 2012, at 16:58 hours, the witness to this sighting was vacationing on a beach near Marseille, France, and noticed many lenticular clouds over the nearby mountains. The witness took several photos of the clouds with a mobile phone and, when reviewing the photos, noticed a black, orb-like UFO in all of them.

Evidence Submitted: Five photos of the UFO.

Initial Action: The team opened this UFO investigation by treating the phenomenon as an AN1: an anomaly that left temporary physical effects, such as lights in the sky and similar phenomena. The team's preliminary analysis of the photo indicated the UFO was, more than likely, dirt on the camera's interior optics.

Investigation and Findings: The witness to this sighting did not speak English. After consultation with OVNI France, a UFO research group in France, the team determined that the witness did not see the UFO in the sky while taking the photos. The witness noticed the UFO later, while reviewing the photos. During their photo analysis, the investigators noticed that regardless of where the witness had pointed the camera or what zoom factor she had used, the UFO always appeared in the same location in the photo. Investigators also conducted a cross-examination of the witness's photos, measuring them against several other photos taken with dirt placed deliberately on the camera sensor. Based on the results of the investigation, the team concluded the UFO was dirt on the camera's internal optics.

Object Details: Dust or dirt on a camera's internal optics will show up as small gray or black spots in photos. More often than not, such spots will show up most clearly in the portions of an image that contain either sky or solid white areas.

Investigator note: dust or dirt on the camera lens will not appear in the photo due to the distance between the lens and the camera sensor.[13]

CASE: 11-002-CE1

Location: Columbia, MD

Date of Event: 09 Sept. 2011

Description: UFO

Disposition: Unidentified

Findings: Inconclusive

Synopsis: On 9 Sept 2011, at approximately 19:00 hours, a couple was traveling on Route 32 from Washington, D.C., to Baltimore, MD, when they saw "a strange craft" they could not explain. Initially, the couple believed the craft was an array of balloons tied together to a flat platform. As the couple got closer to the craft, they could clearly see it did not have balloons. To avoid a traffic accident, the couple stopped the car on the Little Patuxent Parkway and monitored the craft as it floated across the highway. They determined the craft continued to travel west for five minutes; at that point, it moved too far away for the couple to continue monitoring it.

Evidence Submitted: A computer-rendered sketch.

Initial Action: The team opened this UFO case as a CE1: a close encounter of a UFO within 500 feet. Given that the sighting occurred near Fort Meade, the National Security Agency, and an array of classified defense contractor facilities, the team's preliminary analysis of the sketch indicated the UFO might have been a man-made, experimental aerial object.

Investigation and Findings: On 24 Sept 11, an investigator met with the two witnesses to this sighting. The two witnesses provided the investigator with a sketch of the UFO they observed and additional information regarding the sighting. The UFO, according to the witnesses, was moving very slowly and silently; it was flat on the bottom; it had several square protrusions with bases on the platform; and the protrusions appeared as if they were an array of black geometric blocks stacked on top of each other. The craft was about four feet high and four feet across, and it seemed to be moving in a purposeful flight pattern.

The team conducted a two-month investigation, which included performing indices checks on MUFON/NUROC databases and searching for relevant information in local Maryland news and media reports, FAA news and events, and NASA news and events. The team also searched the military news and events reports for all military and defense contractor facilities in the area where the UFO was sighted. When the team completed the investigative process, the object, although possibly man-made, remain unidentified.

Object Details: Unidentified.

CASE: 12-001-CE1

Location: Niagara Falls, Canada

Date of Event: 14 Oct. 08

Description: Men in Black

Disposition: Unidentified

Findings: Inconclusive

Synopsis: On 14 Oct. 08, at approximately 22:30 hours, two witnesses were standing outside of their hotel. They saw a large, triangular UFO with three white lights on each side; it had a pulsing red light in the middle of the craft. The UFO flew from east to west until it was completely out of sight.

Several weeks later, according to three other witnesses, two unidentified Men in Black (MIB) visited the same hotel; they were looking for the two witnesses who had seen the UFO. Although the two witnesses were not at the hotel at the time, the MIB harassed the hotel staff for approximately thirty minutes. The MIB then left the hotel and never returned.[14]

Evidence Submitted: Surveillance footage of the MIB.

Initial Action: The team opened this UFO case as a CE1: a close encounter of a UFO within 500 feet. The team's preliminary analysis of the MIB report indicated a possible hoax.

Investigation and Findings: The investigators interviewed all of the witness multiple times; the witnesses were judged to be reliable, and the investigators had no evidence at the time to suggest the contrary. The investigators also knew of numerous UFO reports regarding this type of UFO sighting along the U.S. and Canadian border, specifically during much of 2008 in the Niagara Falls area. Many of these UFO reports described a black, triangular craft with three bright lights on its edges and a pulsing red light in the middle.

Since there had been other, similar sightings of and reports about the same UFO, the investigators concluded the witnesses did see an actual, unknown aerial object. However, the investigators could find no physical proof, beyond a reasonable doubt, to suggest the black triangle was of extraterrestrial origin. Furthermore, the investigators conducted multiple telephone interviews with the witnesses working at the hotel who had personally spoken with the MIB. The firsthand testimony of these witnesses corroborated the MIB story related by the primary witnesses. However, the investigators found no proof to conclude whether or not the MIB were associated with the UFO report or, for that matter, whether the event was a hoax.

Object Details: Unidentified.

CASE: 11-004-AN2

Location: Jarrettsville Pike, MD

Date of Event: 06 June 2011

Description: Crop Circle

Disposition: Identified

Findings: Farming Equipment

Synopsis: On 06 June 2011, the witness to this sighting reported seeing crop circles in the wheat fields near Jarrettsville Pike, close to the intersection of Blenheim Rd., north of the Loch Raven Watershed. Other than the location of the alleged crop circle, the witness provided no additional information.

Evidence Submitted: The location of the crop circle.

Initial Action: The team opened this UFO case as an AN2: an anomaly that left lasting physical effects, such as crop circles, scorched earth, and debris.

Investigation and Findings: The investigators traveled to the wheat fields in the vicinity of Jarrettsville Pike and took dozens of photographs of the alleged crop circles. After their interview with the owner of the farm, they concluded the markings on the wheat field were a result of farming equipment.

Object Details: Identified as markings made by farming equipment.

CASE: 11-005-MA1

Location: Chesapeake, VA

Date of Event: 10 Sept. 2011

Description: UFO

Disposition: Identified

Findings: Man-Made; Hoax

Synopsis: On 10 Sept. 2011, at 15:14 hours, the witness to this sighting took a photo of a black UFO hovering over the Chesapeake area. The witness reported that the UFO zigzagged across the sky and made quick turns.

Evidence Submitted: A photo of the UFO.

Initial Action: The team opened this UFO case as an MA1: a visual sighting of a UFO that traveled in a discontinuous trajectory, which could mean making loops, quick turns, or vast changes in altitude. The team's preliminary analysis of the photo indicated a possible hoax.

Investigation and Findings: The investigators quickly identified this UFO as hoax for a variety of reasons. After conducting a pixel analysis of the photo, investigators determined the object was embedded into the photo; their review of multiple open-source websites indicated the witness had associations with several UFO conspiracy organizations and had joked about the fake UFO photo he submitted. Furthermore, the team's indices checks revealed the witness to be a professional photographer, which required the team to apply additional scrutiny to the photograph. The witness did not respond to any interview requests from the investigators of this case.

Object Details: Hoax

CASE: 11-006-MA1

Location: Hoboken, NJ

Date of Event: 18 Sept. 2011

Description: UFO

Disposition: Identified

Findings: Balloons

Synopsis: On 18 Sept. 2011, while observing a jetliner flying over Hoboken, the witness to this sighting spotted a bright object that appeared motionless. The object was directly above the witness at a high altitude, far above the clouds. The witness observed the object for about three minutes to see if it was stationary, comparing it to a nearby building. Using a Canon digital camera and a tripod, the witness took 12 consecutive photos of the UFO until it completely moved behind the cloud coverage.

Evidence Submitted: Twelve photos of the UFO.

Initial Action: The team opened this UFO case as an MA1: a visual sighting of a UFO that traveled in a discontinuous trajectory, which could mean making loops, quick turns, or vast changes in altitude. The team's preliminary analysis of the photo indicated the presence of balloons.

Investigation and Findings: The investigators interviewed the witness to this sighting multiple times. The investigators researched military high-altitude "persistence surveillance" balloons and blimps to determine the primary object of the investigation. According to the team's research, the Lakehurst to Picatinny, NJ, corridor is home to an array of classified defense contractors competing for Department of Defense aerial surveillance drones and blimps. According to open-source documents, several defense contractors at Lakehurst test high-altitude, inflatable drones. When all investigative efforts were exhausted, the team determined the object was nothing more than helium party balloons.

Object Details: Balloons.

CASE: 11-009-FB1

Location: Pylesville, MD

Date of Event: 17 Oct. 2011

Description: UFO

Disposition: Identified

Findings: Military Blimp

Synopsis: On 17 Oct. 2011, at approximately 16:30 hours, the witness to this sighting noticed a "weird-looking blimp" in the sky. The witness claimed the object appeared to be a blimp that was shaped like a worm. The object, according to the witness, appeared to be spinning and reflecting the sunlight off its gray surface. The sunlight, however, prevented the witness from seeing the actual surface of the craft. After a few minutes, the UFO moved out of sight.

Evidence Submitted: None.

Initial Action: The team opened this UFO case as an FB1: a fly-by of a UFO that traveled in a straight line across the sky. The team's preliminary analysis of the report indicated an airship (that is, a blimp).

Investigation and Findings: The investigators interviewed the witness to this sighting and determined the object was indeed a blimp, not some other type of craft. After their interview, the investigators conducted further research and analysis of the types of blimps that could be operating in the area. The investigators found a photo of the Argus One airship created by the World Surveillance Group, Inc. The company, which develops surveillance blimps for the military, has a testing facility in nearby Easton, Maryland. The team provided the witness with photos of the Argus One airship for comparison; subsequently, the witness agreed it was what he had seen.

Object Details: As of the writing of this book, Airship Argus One was a new airship design. The Argus One came equipped with a newly developed stabilization system and an integrated payload bay capable of initially carrying up to approximately thirty pounds of high technology sensors, cameras, or electronics packages.[15]

CASE: 11-015-FB1

Location: Davidsonville, MD

Date of Event: 08 Nov. 2011

Description: UFO

Disposition: Identified

Findings: Man-Made Object

Synopsis: On 8 Nov. 2011, at 20:30 hours, the witness to this sighting looked at a cornfield and noticed a large, black triangular UFO flying low. The UFO changed directions and tilted toward where the witness was standing. The witness claimed the UFO was a black triangle that made little noise. According to the witness, the black triangle had three distinct white lights on each corner, a green light on one corner, and a red light on the opposite corner. The UFO flew along Governors Bridge Road toward Route 50 until it was no longer within sight.

Evidence Submitted: A computer-rendered sketch.

Initial Action: The team opened this UFO case as an FB1: a fly-by of a UFO that traveled in a straight line across the sky. The team's preliminary analysis of the report indicated a possible drone, perhaps the X-47B, which operates in the Maryland area.

Investigation and Findings: The investigators traveled to Davidsonville and interviewed the witness to this sighting. The witness, who was the owner of the cornfield, alleged that the UFO flew over the cornfield for an unknown amount of time until it flew north toward Route 50. After the interview, the investigators conducted extensive research regarding man-made triangular aircrafts and drones that were being tested in the Maryland area. Given the description of the UFO, and that the green and red lights were likely FAA navigation beacons, the object was, more than likely, an aircraft from the Patuxent Naval Air Station, which was testing several UAVs in the area.

Object Details: Identified as an aircraft, type unknown.

CASE: 12-051-CE3

Location: Omaha, NE

Date of Event: 02 March 2012

Description: Alien Entity

Disposition: Identified

Findings: Pareidolia

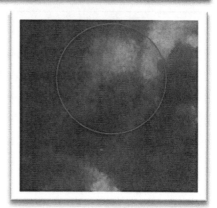

Synopsis: On the night of 2 March 2012, the witness to this sighting was in a bedroom conducting a paranormal investigation. During a photo and electronic voice phenomena (EVP) session, the witness purportedly captured an image of an extraterrestrial on a camera and an instance of a possible extraterrestrial attempting to communicate. The witness reported that another person in the same home saw an unidentified entity in his room and a UFO hovering over a neighbor's home.

Evidence Submitted: Five photos of the extraterrestrial entity and an audio recording of the extraterrestrial's voice.

Initial Action: The team opened this UFO case as a CE3: a visual sighting of an extraterrestrial entity. Initial e-mails from the witness indicated pareidolia and hysteria.

Investigation and Findings: The investigators interviewed the witness to this sighting on several occasions. According to the witness, all efforts to gain media attention regarding the extraterrestrial entity and the UFO failed. Over a dozen e-mails and several phone calls from the witness indicated the witness was experiencing pareidolia and, perhaps, hysteria. Additionally, the witness indicated the home where the photo and EVPs were taken was a former funeral home. After conducting the interview, the team forwarded the investigation results to several paranormal groups, which concluded in their own investigations that the entity was neither extraterrestrial nor paranormal. The team closed the investigation due to a lack of information suggesting the case was related to UFOs.

Object Details: Pareidolia.

CASE: 12-058-CE5

Location: Timonium, MD

Date of Event: 29 July 2011

Description: Alien Implant

Disposition: Unidentified

Findings: Inconclusive

Synopsis: On or about 29 July 2011, while vacationing at a condominium with his family in Ocean City, MD, the witness to this incident awoke from a very realistic dream to find a blue-colored, furry, "troll-looking creature" crouched down beside his bed looking at him. When he fully awoke, at approximately 08:00 hours, he went to the bathroom. At this point, he looked down at his left arm and found an odd-shaped, metallic object partially imbedded in his arm. The witness extracted the object easily and decided to have it analyzed. He put it in a Ziploc bag and placed the bag on the bedroom counter; then, he placed his wallet over the bag. The next day, when he went to examine the object, he found it was missing. The edge of the bag was "burnt out" at one corner.

Evidence Submitted: A sketch of the extraterrestrial entity and the Ziploc bag in which the alleged extraterrestrial implant was stored.

Initial Action: The team opened this UFO case as a CE5: an encounter in which an abducted witness suffers physical or psychological injuries or death.

Investigation and Findings: The investigators traveled to Timonium and interviewed the witness to this sighting. During the interview, and in subsequent e-mail communication, the witness could not recall the exact date upon which the event took place. This uncertainty made it difficult for the investigators to gather exact facts for the investigation (i.e., weather conditions, data about other reported sightings in the area during the timeframe, and so forth). The lead investigator checked other sightings reported in the Ocean City area that took place during the mid-July to early-August period of 2011 and could find nothing that corresponded to this witness's claim. The lead investigator also checked information about other types of reported alien implants and found nothing that corresponded to the witness's description of the artifact he found in his arm.

The lead investigator also interviewed (via phone) the witness's father, a medical doctor who was present at the vacation condominium during this incident. The father stated that he felt his son had merely had a very realistic dream, and that the artifact found in his son's arm was actually a mundane sliver of shaving metal that had been overlooked until the morning of the reported incident. The lead investigator asked the father if he felt his son was prone to lie or exaggerate, and the father said no; instead, he believed his son was mistaking a dream for reality. Lastly, the team conducted forensic analysis of the Ziploc bag, including standard luminol testing and burn replication, and did not find any traces of blood or any chemical residue that would explain the burned hole in the bag.

Object Details: Unidentified

CASE: 12-045-CE3

Location: North Port, FL

Date of Event: 30 Jan. 2011

Description: Alien Entity

Disposition: Unidentified

Findings: Hoax

Synopsis: On 30 Jan. 2011, at 22:00 hours, the witness to this sighting was lying down on a bed and felt a usual weight on the bed. Since the witness's dog likes to sleep on the bed, the witness assumed that accounted for the weight. However, when the witness called the dog's name, there was no response. The witness became instantly fearful and quickly realized that whatever was on the bed was not the dog after all. The witness grabbed a cell phone and quickly snapped a picture of an alien entity under the blanket. The next thing the witness remembered was sitting in the living room and looking at the picture on the phone. The witness could not remember moving from the bedroom to the living room.

Evidence Submitted: A photo of an alleged extraterrestrial.

Initial Action: The team opened this UFO case as a CE3: a visual sighting of an extraterrestrial entity. The team's initial analysis of the photo proved inconclusive.

Investigation and Findings: The investigators made several attempts to interview the witness regarding the photo and to obtain a copy of the original photo for analysis. The witness, however, provided multiple excuses about why she would not provide information to the investigators and soon cut contact with the investigators. The team performed additional background checks, which indicated the witness had attempted to gain media attention regarding the incident. Given that the witness would not provide the original photo for analysis and had attempted to gain media attention, the team closed the investigation as unidentified and possibly a hoax.

Object Details: Unidentified and possibly a hoax.

CASE: 12-044-AN1

Location: Baltimore, MD

Date of Event: 29 June 2012

Description: UFO

Disposition: Identified

Findings: Power-Line Fire

Synopsis: On 29 June 2012, at 23:30 hours, the witness to this sighting reported seeing a bright red-and-orange orb that appeared to be descending from the middle of the sky and disappeared behind the trees.

Evidence Submitted: Video and photo of the orb.

Initial Action: The team opened this UFO investigation by treating the phenomenon as an AN1: an anomaly that left temporary physical effects, such as lights in the sky and similar phenomena. The team's preliminary analysis of the photo indicated the UFO was, more than likely, a power-line explosion. During the exact date and time of this event, a severe thunderstorm with winds up to sixty knots caused massive damage to infrastructure in the Baltimore area, causing considerable amounts of power outages, fallen trees, and downed power lines.

Investigation and Findings: On 8 July 2012, the investigators traveled to Baltimore and interviewed the witness. The team deemed the witness to be credible and determined she displayed no signs of deception. After the interview, the investigators visited the approximate location where the orb had descended. While on site, the investigators saw multiple downed trees and power lines, which were results of the severe thunderstorm. The team conducted additional research regarding power-line explosions and fires, and they compared photos of known power-line fires. After completing their research, they concluded the UFO the witness had observed was a power-line explosion.

Object Details: During a severe storm, flying debris, lighting, and downed tree limbs can cause power lines to catch fire. In some instances, the transformers attached to the poles can also explode and give the appearance of large, glowing, red-and-orange orbs.

CASE: 12-042-AN1

Location: Whiteford, MD

Date of Event: 06 June 2012

Description: UFO

Disposition: Identified

Findings: Artificial Satellite

Synopsis: On 6 June 2012, at approximately 23:37 hours, the witness to this sighting was walking the family dog and observed a bright, star-like object in the sky traveling west to east. According to the witness, "the UFO" was traveling very fast in a straight line.

Evidence Submitted: Video footage from a cellphone.

Initial Action: The team opened this UFO investigation by treating the phenomenon as an AN1: an anomaly that left temporary physical effects, such as lights in the sky and similar phenomena. The team's preliminary analysis of the photo indicated the UFO was, more than likely, an artificial satellite in LEO.

Investigation and Findings: The investigators contacted the witness to this sighting. According to the witness, the UFO was a star-like object that made no noise; it also traveled in a straight path and made no erratic maneuvers. The team performed indices checks on satellite tracking databases, which later indicated the UFO was the Iridium 44 communications satellite in LEO. The Iridium 44 satellite passed over the witness at nearly the same time as the time the witness reported seeing the UFO.

Object Details: The Iridium 44 is part of a planned commercial communications network comprised of a constellation of sixty-six LEO spacecraft. The satellite launched from China on 8 Dec. 1997 and remains in LEO with an apogee of 654 km and a perigee of 629 km.[16]

AERIAL PHENOMENA

CASE: 11-038-FB1

Location: Buffalo, NY

Date of Event: 05 June 2011

Description: UFO

Disposition: Identified

Findings: Aircraft

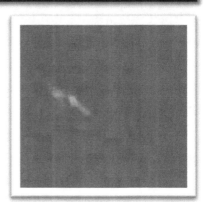

Synopsis: On 5 June 2011, while testing a new high-definition video camera, the witness to this sighting recorded a UFO in the sky. The witness, however, did not observe the UFO firsthand and only noticed the UFO when reviewing the footage later at home.

Evidence Submitted: Video footage from a Camcorder.

Initial Action: The team opened this UFO investigation by treating the phenomenon as an FB1: a fly-by of a UFO that traveled in a straight line across the sky. The team's preliminary analysis of the report indicated a possible airplane flying to Buffalo International Airport.

Investigation and Findings: While interviewing the witness, the investigators learned that the footage had been taken during a soccer game held near Buffalo. After the interview, the investigators enhanced the photo using Canon Professional Photo Edition software. When examining the enhanced photo, investigators found a commercial aircraft illuminated by a sun flare. The enhanced image revealed a wingspan and tail rudder. Additionally, investigators conducted research regarding aircraft illuminated by sun flares and found several photos that resembled the image in the video captured by the witness to this sighting. The investigators concluded the object the witness had captured on camera was an aircraft heading to Buffalo International Airport.

Object Details: A commercial or military aircraft.

CASE: 12-034-AN1

Location: Grimsby, U.K.

Date of Event: 12 May 2012

Description: UFO

Disposition: Unidentified

Findings: Inconclusive

Synopsis: On 12 May 2012, at 21:30 hours, an infrared camera took a photo of a UFO near Grimsby. The UFO was captured on a Forscam infrared webcam mounted on the roof of the witness's home.

Evidence Submitted: Infrared video footage of the UFO.

Initial Action: The team opened this UFO investigation by treating the phenomenon as an AN1: an anomaly that left temporary physical effects, such as lights in the sky and similar phenomena. The team's preliminary analysis of the photo indicated the UFO was, more than likely, an insect captured on the webcam.

Investigation and Findings: The investigators conducted multiple interviews with the witness to this sighting. The investigators conducted open-source research for orb-related activity in Grimsby, which resulted in finding an abundant number of photos and videos of orb activity in England. However, the investigators could find no explanation, other than the presence of Chinese lanterns, for these sightings. The investigators attempted to shape the investigation toward an optic event or an insect as the culprit. According to the team's research, orbs are typically circular artifacts that occur in flash photography—sometimes they are accompanied by trails indicating motion. Photographers capture orb artifacts during low-light instances in which the camera's flash is used, such as at night. "Purple fringing" (PF), moreover, is the term photographers use to describe an out-of-focus purple or magenta "ghost" image on a photograph.[17]

However, the investigators could not conclude that the orb was definitely a result of PF. Therefore, they contacted the U.K. Royal Entomology Society to determine if the society could identify the object as a possible insect. The members of the Royal Entomology Society shared the opinion that the orb could not have been a known insect. The team had exhausted the investigative process, so they closed the investigation as "unidentified."

Object Details: Unidentified.

CASE: 12-024-FB1

Location: Hoboken, NJ

Date of Event: 14 Apr. 2012

Description: UFO

Disposition: Identified

Findings: Gold Party Balloon

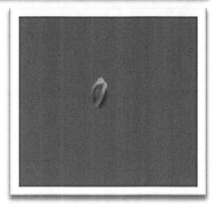

Synopsis: On 14 Apr. 2012, at 16:30 hours, the witness to this sighting was sitting outside a condominium complex. The witness saw a metallic-gold UFO in the sky. According to the witness, the UFO was shaped like a donut and appeared to be dragging a line or string.

Evidence Submitted: Thirteen photos of the UFO.

Initial Action: The team opened this UFO investigation by treating the phenomenon as an FB1: a fly-by of a UFO that traveled in a straight line across the sky. The team's preliminary analysis of the report indicated a possible balloon or blimp.

Investigation and Findings: According to the witness, the UFO was metallic gold and was moving along with the wind. The UFO appeared to have been dragging a string or a rope. The investigators took a tour of the Hoboken area, found a party store named "Party City," and purchased a "Zero Gold Helium Balloon," which was identical to the

UFO photographed by the witness. The investigators concluded the UFO was nothing more than a party balloon.

Object Details: A gold helium balloon.

CASE: 12-019-AN1

Location: Atlantic Ocean

Date of Event: 5 Jan. 2012

Description: UFO

Disposition: Identified

Findings: Lens Flare

Synopsis: On 5 Jan. 2012, at approximately 18:41 hours, the witness to this sighting was on board the cruise ship *MSC Poesia*, which was heading back to Florida. The witness, who was in cabin 11151, went outside and onto the balcony to take a photo of the sunset. Upon reviewing the photo, the witness claimed to see a UFO.

Evidence Submitted: A photo of the UFO.

Initial Action: The team opened this UFO investigation by treating the phenomenon as an AN1: an anomaly that left temporary physical effects, such as lights in the sky and similar phenomena. The team's preliminary analysis of the video indicated the UFO was, more than likely, a catadioptric lens flare.

Investigation and Findings: During an interview with investigators, the witness explained that he did not personally observe the UFO while taking photos of the sky, which investigators recognized as a common indicator of a lens flare. In an effort to positively identify the object as a lens flare, investigators obtained the original photo and applied standard cross-section analysis to it. Their analysis of the photo indicated the anomaly had intersected with the sun inside the frame of view, creating a lens flare.

Object Details: Lens flares are created when non-image-forming light enters the camera lens and subsequently hit the camera's film or digital sensor.[18] The lens flare often appears as a polygonal shape, giving the appearance of a "flying disk or saucer."

CASE: 12-015-CE5

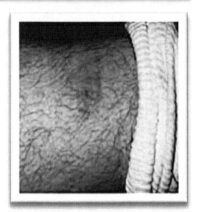

Location: Wash. Township, NJ

Date of Event: 24 Feb. 02

Description: Alien Abduction

Disposition: Unresolved

Findings: Likely Pareidolia

Synopsis: The witness to this sighting contacted API alleging to have been abducted by extraterrestrials, experiencing three and a half minutes of missing time and suffering from bruising and marks on the leg. The witness's other physical complaints included ringing in the ears and mysterious bloodstains on the sheets, which the witness discovered upon waking up from sleep. According to the witness, physicians had completed an ultrasound on the bruised area. The findings, allegedly, revealed an unknown mass under the area and tendons that had been cut and removed, as if surgery had been conducted.

Evidence Submitted: Photos of scars and an image of an ultrasound.

Initial Action: The team opened this UFO case by treating the phenomenon as a CE5: an encounter in which an abducted witness suffers physical or psychological injuries or death. The team's initial research indicated the witness had associations with conspiracy groups and had dedicated a website, as well as other social media, to the subject.

Investigation and Findings: After the witness reported the case to several UFO organizations, MUFON contacted the witness in November 2010; MUFON representatives believed a hypnotic regression session was warranted. The witness failed to follow up and attend the indicated sessions due to personal issues. Nevertheless, the witness continued to speak openly and publicly about the experience, even presenting at several UFO conferences. However, the witness always had reservations about doing a hypnotic regression session.

During this investigation, the team interviewed the witness on three separate occasions; in each, the witness revealed no new information relevant to the MUFON case. Although the witness provided no physical proof to substantiate the claims, the lead investigator formed the opinion that the witness was experiencing a high degree of pareidolia and anxiety. The team could not rule out the possibility of a hoax. The team exhausted all investigative efforts and closed the case as "unresolved."

Object Details: Abduction claims were unresolved; object in the leg remained unidentified.

CASE: 12-008-AN1

Location: Tempe, AZ

Date of Event: 18 July 2010

Description: UFO

Disposition: Identified

Findings: Clouds

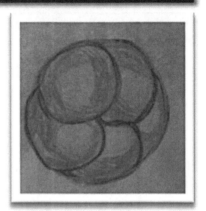

Synopsis: On 18 July 2010, at approximately 20:00 hours, the witness to this sighting was standing on a second floor patio. The witness noticed a strange object hovering about 200 feet over the city of Tempe. The witness described the object as giving off heat and looked like a white-and-orange jellyfish. The object actively morphed in color and appeared as though it had a circular membrane. The object hovered over the city for approximately fifteen minutes and then it moved slowly from east to west.

Evidence Submitted: A sketch of the UFO.

Initial Action: The team opened this UFO investigation by treating the phenomenon as an AN1: an anomaly that left temporary physical effects, such as lights in the sky and similar phenomena. The team's initial analysis of the report indicated the cause was a likely natural phenomenon, based upon knowledge of severe thunderstorms on the same date and time as when the witness observed the UFO.

Investigation and Findings: The investigators traveled to Phoenix and interviewed the witness to this sighting. During the interview, the witness provided the investigators with a sketch of the UFO. Additionally, the investigators learned that the witness had been drinking alcohol when she spotted the UFO. The lead investigator noted the witness appeared sincere and credible. During the portion of the team's investigation that focused on weather research and analysis, the team determined that the data indicated the witness had observed a convergence of several natural phenomena: Rayleigh scattering during sunset, high temperatures, and severe thunderstorms, all of which converged with altocumulus castellanus cloud formations.

Object Details: When sunlight passes through a thick layer of atmosphere and dust particles at sunset, Rayleigh Scattering (see glossary) takes place, scattering the blue color and ensuring only red-to-orange color remains. The clouds reflect these unscattered red and/or orange rays, appearing in that color. More importantly, during high temperatures and an approaching thunderstorm, the orange clouds would appear even more prominent.[19]

CASE: 12-008-FB1

Location: Hidden Valley, CA

Date of Event: 13 Oct. 2009

Description: UFO

Disposition: Identified

Findings: Spider Silk

Synopsis: On 13 Oct. 2009, while taking photos of flowers in a garden, the witness to this sighting inadvertently took two photographs of a "fast-moving UFO."

Evidence Submitted: Two photos of a UFO.

Initial Action: The team opened this UFO investigation by treating the phenomenon as an FB1: a fly-by of a UFO that traveled in a straight line across the sky.

Investigation and Findings: The investigators conducted multiple interviews with the witness to this sighting. The witness provided the investigators with the original photographs, which were taken with a Kodak CX7530. The investigators extracted the EXIF data from the photographs and examined the objects in the images closely. The team's analytical conclusion strongly indicated the streaks were close to the camera; thus, the streaks could not represent a contrail. During subsequent photo analysis, the team concluded the streak was a piece of spider silk in the foreground that was catching the sunlight.

Object Details: Silk from a spiderweb.

CASE: 12-007-FB1

Location: Rhodesia, Africa

Date of Event: Circa 1953

Description: UFO

Disposition: Unidentified

Findings: Inconclusive

Synopsis: In 1953 (the exact day or month is unknown), the witness to this sighting saw a large, silver-colored flying disk in Rhodesia. The witness, who admitted the event had occurred over sixty years ago, could still remember the event vividly.

Evidence Submitted: A sketch of the UFO.

Initial Action: The team opened this UFO investigation by treating the phenomenon as an FB1: a fly-by of a UFO that traveled in a straight line across the sky.

Investigation and Findings: The investigators interviewed the witness to this sighting, whom they deemed credible. The witness is a lawyer and author of many novels. According to the witness, while outside the local post office in Salisbury, he saw a silver-colored, disk-shaped UFO hovering over the city. The UFO hovered for about five minutes and then "shot straight up into the air" until it was no longer in sight.

The investigators contacted a local newspaper, *The Herald*, in Zimbabwe in hopes of retrieving archived reports that would corroborate the witness's testimony. However, the newspaper editor could not provide any information because the country's Civil War had resulted in destruction of the newspaper's archives. Because the sighting had taken place nearly fifty-five years prior to the investigation, and in a remote country, the investigators could not find a sufficient amount of relevant information with which to identify the object. Therefore, they closed the investigation as "unresolved and unidentified."

Object Details: Unidentified.

CASE: 12-004-FB1

Location: Baltimore, MD

Date of Event: 31 Dec. 2011

Description: UFO Fleet

Disposition: Identified

Findings: Chinese Lanterns

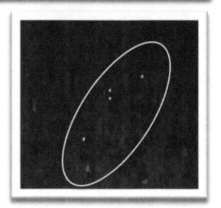

Synopsis: On 31 Dec. 2011, at 23:45 hours, three separate witnesses were celebrating New Year's Eve in downtown Baltimore. While smoking cigarettes outside in a yard, the witnesses saw three orange lights, which were shaped in a pyramid, in the sky. The three lights slowly rotated clockwise, paused briefly, and started rotating counterclockwise. Then, the lights split off and descended into the distance in three separate directions.

Evidence Submitted: A photo of the three orange orbs and video footage taken from a hand-held Camcorder.

Initial Action: The team opened this UFO investigation by treating the phenomenon as an FB1: a fly-by of a UFO that traveled in a straight line across the sky. Given that the event had occurred only several minutes before midnight on New Year's Eve, and the event had occurred in a large city, the team's initial indication was that the three lights were some type of celebratory fireworks or Chinese lanterns.

Investigation and Findings: The investigators traveled to Baltimore and interviewed the three witnesses. The witnesses seemed sincere and appeared to be truthful. One of the witnesses described the sight as if there had been "a lit flame flickering within the orbs." During the investigation, the investigators traveled to the area where the three orbs had vanished from sight, but they found no ground traces to suggest the orbs were fireworks. After conducting weather analysis for the time and date at which the orbs were sighted, the investigators determined the wind had been blowing in the same direction as the one the orbs traveled in. Given the description of the orbs, the direction they traveled, the fact it was New Year's Eve, and that the orbs had slowly "turned off," the investigators concluded the objects were some type of celebratory Chinese lanterns.

Object Details: Chinese lanterns.

CASE: 12-006-FB1

Location: Buffalo, MO

Date of Event: Late July 1999

Description: UFO

Disposition: Unidentified

Findings: Inconclusive

Synopsis: In late July 1999, at approximately 03:30 hours, the witness to this sighting was camping on a hilltop near Buffalo (in the Ozark Mountains). While keeping warm near the campfire, the witness saw an egg-shaped, glowing UFO that was "fire-orange" in color. The UFO, according to the witness, was silent and hovered in the area for forty-five minutes. The UFO moved slowly from east to west until it was no longer in sight.

Evidence Submitted: A sketch of the UFO.

Initial Action: The team opened this UFO investigation by treating the phenomenon as an FB1: a fly-by of a UFO that traveled in a straight line across the sky.

Investigation and Findings: The investigators interviewed the witness to this sighting. The lead investigator formed the opinion that the witness was sincere and credible. The team performed several indices checks on open-source websites, in particular MUFON/NUFORC; these checks provided the team with information showing similarities to this UFO sighting. However, because the sighting had taken place at a remote location nearly thirteen years before the investigation, the investigators could not find a sufficient amount of relevant information they could use to identify the object. Therefore, they closed the investigation as "unresolved and unidentified."

Object Details: Unidentified.

AERIAL PHENOMENA

CASE: 12-031-AN1

Location: Great Falls, VA

Date of Event: 02 March 2012

Description: UFO

Disposition: Identified

Findings: The Moon

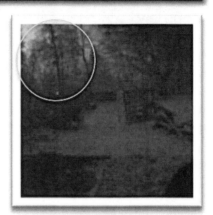

Synopsis: On 2 March 2012, at 23:21 hours, an infrared webcam took several photos of a UFO hovering in a backyard. According to the owner of the webcam, the UFO must have been silent because the event did not wake up the webcam owner's family.

Evidence Submitted: An infrared photo of a light in the background of a scene.

Initial Action: The team opened this UFO investigation by treating the phenomenon as an AN1: an anomaly that left temporary physical effects, such as lights in the sky and similar phenomena. The team's initial analysis of the report indicated the range of the infrared camera was too short to be triggered by an aerial object in the sky. More than likely, the team believed, the camera had been triggered by something closer to the home, and the light in the background was from the moon.

Investigation and Findings: On 29 March 2012, the investigators traveled to Great Falls and interviewed the witness to this sighting. The investigators, along with the witness, took a tour of the backyard; specifically, they examined the area at which the webcam had been pointing. The investigators noticed a very large hole in the surrounding fence and deer feces directly in front of the webcam. Given that the range of the webcam's sensor was short, the investigators determined it likely an animal had triggered the camera. In response, the camera had taken a poor-quality photo of the moon in the background. The investigators also noted that on the night of this incident, the moon was at the waxing gibbous stage, with an illumination factor of 66%.

Object Details: An animal triggered the camera, which took a photo of the moon.

CASE: 12-032-FB1

Location: Lawrence, KS

Date of Event: 21 Aug. 2011

Description: UFO

Disposition: Unidentified

Findings: Inconclusive

Synopsis: On 21 Aug. 2011, at approximately 17:30 hours, the witness to this sighting was driving home from work. The witness spotted a solid, black object hovering in the sky. The unidentified object, according to the witness, must have been 500 feet up. The witness watched the unidentified object remain in a stationary position and hover for at least thirty seconds. The witness turned away for a brief moment, only to turn back and notice the unidentified object was gone.

Evidence Submitted: A computer-rendered sketch of the UFO.

Initial Action: The team opened this UFO investigation by treating the phenomenon as an FB1: a fly-by of a UFO that traveled in a straight line across the sky.

Investigation and Findings: The investigator interviewed the witness to this sighting and found him to seem sincere and truthful. However, the investigator performed several indices checks on open-source websites (in particular, on MUFON/NUFORC), and these checks provided the investigator with no information regarding this sighting. The investigator could not find relevant information (UFO reporting data, weather reports, military activity reports, defense contractor activities, or NASA or other space flight activities, etc.) with which to identify the object. Therefore, the investigator closed the investigation as "unresolved and unidentified."

Object Details: Unidentified.

AERIAL PHENOMENA

CASE: 12-002-FB1

Location: Baltimore, MD

Date of Event: 06 Jan. 2012

Description: UFO

Disposition: Identified

Findings: Chinese Lantern

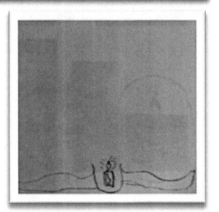

Synopsis: On 6 Jan. 2012, at approximately 21:00 hours, the witness to this sighting was returning to a hotel. The witness saw a "strange object in the sky." According to the witness, the object was circular, had two wings, and appeared to have a flickering amber light in its center. A second witness, who happened to be standing outside the hotel, also saw the object in the sky. While the two witnesses discussed the object, another object, identical to the first, appeared and traveled west until it was no longer in sight.

Evidence Submitted: A sketch of the UFO.

Initial Action: The team opened this UFO investigation by treating the phenomenon as an FB1: a fly-by of a UFO that traveled in a straight line across the sky. Given that the object of the sketch displayed light like a "flickering candle" and it had traveled west, along with the wind, the team determined a type of Chinese lantern was likely the culprit.

Investigation and Findings: The investigators traveled to Baltimore and interviewed the first witness to this sighting. The sketch provided by the witness appeared to show an object with a flame flickering in its center. The object, according to the witness, had moved in the same direction as the wind and at a speed consistent with the weather for that night. The team therefore determined that the object was, more than likely, a type of Chinese lantern or something similar.

Object Details: A type of Chinese lantern.

CASE: 12-033-AN1

Location: Chicago, IL

Date of Event: 27 March 2001

Description: UFO

Disposition: Unidentified

Findings: Inconclusive

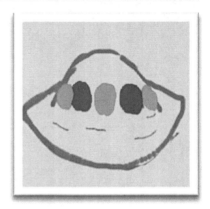

Synopsis: On 27 March 2001, at 03:00 hours, the witness to this sighting was standing near the bedroom window in her home when she observed a disk-shaped UFO hovering over a neighbor's house across the street. The witness ran outside to get a better look, but the UFO was no longer in sight. According to the witness, the UFO had many green and red lights, which gave it the appearance of a Christmas tree.

Evidence Submitted: A sketch of the UFO.

Initial Action: The team opened this UFO investigation by treating the phenomenon as an AN1: an anomaly that left temporary physical effects, such as lights in the sky and similar phenomena.

Investigation and Findings: The investigators interviewed the witness to this sighting, whom they found to be sincere and truthful. According to the witness, the UFO had windows that were bright green and red, a blue strobe, and a blue-white spotlight that had been pointed at the witness's neighbor's home. Although the investigators could not determine what the object was, they did determine the green and red lights could have been associated with FAA navigation lights, while the blue strobe could have been a collision light. Additionally, after performing several indices checks on open-source websites (in particular, MUFON/NUFORC), the team found no information regarding this sighting. Because the sighting had taken place nearly twelve years prior to the investigation, the investigators could not find relevant information (UFO reporting data, weather reports, military activity reports, or NASA reports, etc.) with which to identify the object. They closed the investigation as "unresolved and unidentified."

Object Details: Unidentified.

CASE: 12-073-FB1

Location: Los Angeles, CA

Date of Event: 06 Jan. 2012

Description: UFO

Disposition: Identified

Findings: Helium Balloon

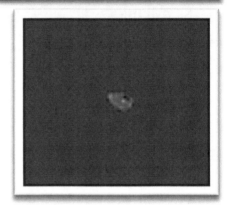

Synopsis: On 6 Jan. 2012, at 18:30 hours, the witness to this sighting was driving through Los Angeles. The witness saw a UFO fly over the city and used a cellphone to record a video of the UFO.

Evidence Submitted: A video of the UFO.

Initial Action: The team opened this UFO case by treating the phenomenon as an FB1: a fly-by of a UFO traveling in a straight line across the sky. The team conducted initial analysis of the video and determined the object was most likely a helium balloon.

Investigation and Findings: The investigators interviewed the witness to this sighting to ensure the video was authentic. They conducted an analysis of the video, which appeared to show a helium balloon flying with the wind. They enabled a super zoom of the video, which clearly showed a string attached to the bottom of a helium balloon. The team closed the case as "resolved and identified."

Object Details: Helium balloon.

CASE: 12-025-MA1

Location: Southern Australia

Date of Event: 14 Apr. 2009

Description: UFO

Disposition: Unresolved

Findings: Unidentified

Synopsis: On 14 Apr. 2009, at 20:00 hours, the witness to this incident claimed to see a red-and-white, glowing orb that was about the size of a small aircraft flying up 600 meters in the sky. The witness stated the night sky was clear and there was nothing else in the sky. The witness further claimed the object was stationary but changed in size from small to large and back to small. The witness stated the object made no sound. The witness claimed the event lasted about fifteen minutes and ended with the object flying upward in a flash, leaving behind a thin streak of light.

Evidence Submitted: A photo of the UFO.

Initial Action: The team opened this UFO case by treating the phenomenon as an MA1: a visual sighting of a UFO that travels in a discontinuous trajectory, which could mean making loops, quick turns, or vast changes in altitude. The team's initial report indicated a possible natural phenomenon, such as a meteor or lightning.

Investigation and Findings: The investigators contacted the witness to this sighting and learned the date of the event was in 2009, not 2012, as the witness had initially reported. The witness was confused about the weather he had observed the night of the sighting and could not recall if the night was clear or not. The team conducted historical weather research on the date, location, and time of the event, and found the data conflicted with the witness's account. The team closed the investigation due to a lack of witness credibility and inconsistent reporting from the witness.

Object Details: Unidentified.

AERIAL PHENOMENA

CASE: 12-021-AN1

Location: Durham, NC

Date of Event: 23 March 2012

Description: UFO

Disposition: Identified

Findings: Man-Made Object

Synopsis: On 23 March 2012, at 01:22 hours, the witness to this sighting was walking along the street. The witness looked up for a moment and saw three very bright lights in the sky. According to the witness, the three lights stretched out slowly, coming together into one larger light. The lights then broke off, traveled out into the distance, and no longer appeared visible in the sky.

Evidence Submitted: A photo of the UFO.

Initial Action: The team opened this UFO case by treating the phenomenon as an AN1: an anomalous object that left no visible sign or traceable evidence. The team's initial report indicated the phenomenon could have been an aircraft from a nearby military base.

Investigation and Findings: The investigator interviewed the witness to this sighting and deemed him sincere and credible. The witness described the lights as appearing like lasers and orbs, but could not capture a good photograph due to the poor quality of the cellphone camera. After several interviews with the witness, the investigators then moved forward into researching government, military, and defense industry activities regarding lasers and plasma balls, which react much like the lights reported by the witness. While researching Northrup Grumman, a company that has two facilities in the same area in which the witness saw the lights, investigators found a video purportedly recording plasma ball testing by Northrup Grumman that was very similar to the one the witness provided. The team gave the witness a copy of the video, and the witness agreed that the lights in the video exactly matched the ones he had seen. The team closed the investigation as "resolved."

Object Details: The lights were explained as results of the process of testing laser technology at Northrup Grumman, a major defense contractor in the Durham area. The company provides space, defense, and electronics systems to an array of U.S. government customers. Its products include military aircraft; satellites for communications; and science, weather, surveillance, and high-energy lasers.[20]

CASE: 12-003-MA1

Location: Lake Villa, IL

Date of Event: Circa 2002

Description: UFO

Disposition: Identified

Findings: Natural Phenomena

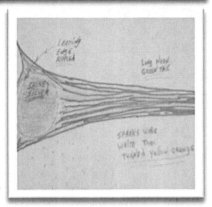

Synopsis: In the autumn of 2002, at sunset, the witness to this sighting noticed a bright green metallic-like sphere flying straight and level. The sphere had a luminescent, green tail. The object was about 50 degrees in elevation at its closest approach and was shedding sparks, which were falling into a group of trees about 300 yards in the distance. The sparks took roughly four seconds to fall into the trees. The witness reported the object had a shiny appearance, like Mercury, and observed ripples in its leading edge. The witness observed the object until it disappeared, moving over the horizon and out of sight; however, the witness did not investigate the trees to look for residue or evidence of burns.

Evidence Submitted: A sketch of the UFO.

Initial Action: The team opened this UFO case by treating the phenomenon as an MA1: a visual sighting of a UFO that traveled in a discontinuous trajectory, which could mean making loops, quick turns, or vast changes in altitude. During the initial stages of this investigation, the investigators noted the witness had submitted multiple UFO reports to MUFON and NUFORC; in these reports, the witness made mention of paranormal and alleged extraterrestrial activity in the vicinity of his home.

Investigation and Findings: This team determined this case had previously been reported to MUFON and NUFORC. When investigating the case further, the team did not find any additional information relevant to the investigation. The team conducted several interviews with the witness, who displayed strong signs of pareidolia. Taking the witness's description at face value, the object was, more than likely, a meteor or re-entering space debris. Furthermore, the team found many reports that were similar to this witness's accounts and that indicated a meteor, including descriptions of the color of the object, the trailing debris, and the angle of flight.

Object Details: A meteor.

CASE: 12-017-FB1

Location: Arlington, VA

Date of Event: 06 June 2006

Description: UFO

Disposition: Identified

Findings: Hoax

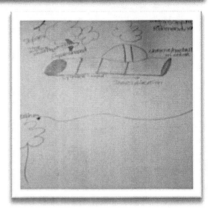

Synopsis: On 6 June 2006, the witness to this sighting was sitting on her front porch. The witness saw a cylinder-shaped UFO moving slowly, then quickly. According to the witness, the UFO traveled in a straight pattern and was much lower than normal aircraft for that area.

Evidence Submitted: A sketch of the UFO.

Initial Action: The team opened this UFO case by treating the phenomenon as an FB1: a fly-by of a UFO traveling in a straight line across the sky.

Investigation and Findings: Although the witness provided a sketch of the UFO, which was identical to many drawings found on the Internet, the witness failed to respond to all the team's requests for an interview and also failed to provide additional information that would clarify the initial report. Moreover, the team performed indices checks on the witness's e-mail account and associated websites, finding evidence of strong pareidolia and associations with conspiracy groups, the occult, and the paranormal. The witness's lack of cooperation, along with her occasional misdirection, led investigators to close the case and classify it as a hoax.

Object Details: Hoax.

CASE: 12-063-FB1

Location: Genesee, MI

Date of Event: Late 1970s

Description: UFO

Disposition: Unidentified

Findings: Unresolved

Synopsis: One day in the late 1970s, at approximately 06:30 hours, the witness to this sighting saw a large UFO hovering over a neighbor's home. According to the witness, the UFO was a silver saucer that had three large white lights and two smaller amber lights; the UFO was completely silent. After the initial sighting, the silver saucer flew straight up into the sky "very fast" until it was no longer in sight.

Evidence Submitted: A sketch of the UFO.

Initial Action: The team opened this UFO investigation by treating the phenomenon as an FB1: a fly-by of a UFO that traveled in a straight line across the sky.

Investigation and Findings: Although the investigators deemed the witness to this sighting credible, they did not have enough information with which to shape the investigation. The investigators conducted several open-source checks to corroborate the witness's story. These checks including examining various UFO databases, astronomical data, weather reports, military activity reports, and NASA reports. Due to the lack of corroboratory data, the team closed the investigation as "unresolved and unidentified."

Object Details: Unidentified.

CASE: 12-065-FB1

Location: Dundalk, MD

Date of Event: 08 Sept. 2012

Description: UFO

Disposition: Identified

Findings: Aircraft

Synopsis: On 8 Sept. 2012, at 20:45 hours, the witness to this sighting was walking toward a neighbor's home and saw a large, orange UFO in the sky. According to the witness, the UFO flew west to east and then southeast at an altitude of about 500 feet. The witness went back inside to retrieve a camera, but when he emerged with the camera, he found the UFO was no longer on site. Several minutes later, another UFO, which had the same appearance as the first, seemed to descend from the clouds and travel in the same direction as the first. The second time this happened, the witness was able to take six photos of the UFO.

Evidence Submitted: Six photos of the UFO.

Initial Action: The team opened this UFO investigation by treating the phenomenon as an FB1: a fly-by of a UFO that traveled in a straight line across the sky.

Investigation and Findings: After several interviews with the witness and exchanging e-mails, the investigator determined that the witness observed several aircraft heading to the nearby Essex Sky Park Airport. According to the weather for the day and time the witness observed the UFOs, there was heavy fog and a completely overcast sky. Moreover, the path upon which the two UFOs traveled (west to east and then southeast) is the normal flight path for aircraft heading to Essex Sky Park Airport. The fog and overcast conditions more than likely gave those aircraft lights the appearance of glowing orbs. Significantly, the witness also displayed signs of hysteria regarding the phenomena, including making the statement that "beings were using inter-dimensional portals to appear and disappear at their pleasure."

Object Details: Aircraft in flight to Essex Sky Park Airport.

CASE: 12-060-CE5

Location: Tulsa, OK

Date of Event: 03 Aug. 2012

Description: Alien Encounters

Disposition: Identified

Findings: Nightmares

Synopsis: The witness to this sighting contacted API after having dreams about aliens. The witness's first dream, which occurred on 3 Aug. 2012, depicted aliens who were slender, gray, and had large black eyes. After the second dream, which occurred on 18 Sept. 2012, the witness woke up but could not move.

Evidence Submitted: A sketch of the alien in the dream.

Initial Action: The team opened this UFO case by treating the phenomenon as a CE5: an encounter in which a witness experiences an abduction.

Investigation and Findings: The team conducted several interviews with the witness and discovered the witness had watched the science fiction movie *The Fourth Kind* prior to having the nightmares. The movie purports to be based on actual events occurring in Nome, Alaska, in 2000, in which psychologist Dr. Abigail Tyler uses hypnosis to uncover her patients' memories of alien abduction.[21] The witness indicted she had no nightmares regarding aliens prior to watching the movie and agreed the alien abduction nightmares were likely a result of the movie. At a final interview with the witness, the witness and investigator agreed that the nightmares more than likely resulted from watching a movie about alien abductions.

Object Details: A nightmare is an unpleasant dream that can cause a strong, negative emotional response from the mind, which is typically fear or horror, but can also be despair, anxiety, or great sadness. The dream may contain situations of danger, discomfort, and psychological or physical terror. Sufferers usually awaken in a state of distress and may be unable to return to sleep for a prolonged period of time.

CASE: 12-067-FB1

Location: Kissimmee, FL

Date of Event: 12 Sept. 2012

Description: UFO

Disposition: Identified

Findings: Bird

Synopsis: The witness to this sighting contacted API regarding a photo he had taken while vacationing at Disney World on 12 Sept. 2012. The witness claimed a UFO could be seen in the photo.

Evidence Submitted: A photo of the UFO.

Initial Action: The team opened this UFO investigation by treating the phenomenon as an FB1: a fly-by of a UFO that traveled in a straight line across the sky.

Investigation and Findings: The investigators interviewed the witness to this sighting and learned that the witness did not personally observe the UFO. The witness noticed the UFO while reviewing the photos later at home. After the interview, the team enhanced the photo using Canon Professional Photo Edition software. When examining the enhanced photo, the team discovered an unidentified bird in flight.

Object Details: Identified as a bird in flight.

CASE: 12-078-FB1

Location: Tampa, FL

Date of Event: 07 Oct. 2012

Description: UFO

Disposition: Identified

Findings: Satellite Flare

Synopsis: On 7 Oct. 2012, while taking photos of the sky at pre-dawn, the witness to this sighting saw a bright object fly overhead in the sky. Initially, the witness thought the object was a satellite, until it became extremely bright. The bright object faded away as it continued to fly away.

Evidence Submitted: A video and photo of the object.

Initial Action: The team opened this UFO investigation by treating the phenomenon as an FB1: a fly-by of a UFO that traveled in a straight line across the sky.

Investigation and Findings: After reviewing the video, the investigators conducted research on various satellite- and meteor-reporting websites. According to several satellite-tracking websites, and the description of the UFO given by the witness, the team determined the UFO was a flare from the Iridium 96 communications satellite.

Object Details: On 11 February 2002, a Delta 2 rocket launched the Iridium 96 communications satellite into LEO. The satellite remains in LEO with an apogee of 682 km and a perigee of 678.3 km.[22]

A satellite flare is caused when the reflective surfaces on satellites (such as antennas or solar panels) reflect sunlight directly onto Earth below; the reflection appears as a brief, bright "flare."

CASE: 11-007-CE3

Location: La Plata, MD

Date of Event: 02 Nov. 2011

Description: Alien Encounter

Disposition: Closed

Findings: Hoax

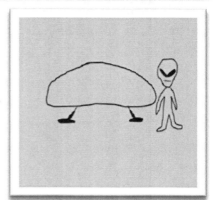

Synopsis: On 2 Nov. 2011, at approximately 18:20 hours, the witness to this sighting reported seeing a medium-sized, metallic UFO in the woods. According to the witness, there were three "human-like aliens near the UFO." The witness described the aliens as gray, saying they had big heads, wore cushioned shoes, and were using a laser to cut out "a heart" from an unidentified animal. When the witness walked toward the aliens, the aliens returned to the UFO, which lifted into the air and "disintegrated into tiny bits." According to the witness, the UFO was silver in color; it had red, blinking lights; and it was shaped like a deep-dish pizza.

Evidence Submitted: A sketch of the UFO.

Initial Action: The team opened this UFO case by treating the phenomenon as a CE3: a visual sighting of a UFO with entities aboard.

Investigation and Findings: The witness's report was written with many misspellings and grammatical errors, which led investigators to believe a child had submitted the UFO report. The lead investigator contacted the La Plata mayor and chief of police for any information regarding this report. According to the chief of police, a search-and-rescue helicopter was in the area at about the same time as the witness observed this event; the helicopter's occupants were searching for a missing person. On the same day as the day of the incident, the Charles Country Sheriff's Department and the Maryland Natural Resources Police found the body of a fifty-two-year-old woman only 5.9 miles from the purported UFO sighting. After finally responding to an interview request, the witness admitted the event was a hoax. The team closed the investigation as such.

Object Details: Hoax.

CASE: 12-007-AN1

Location: Guttenberg, Iowa

Date of Event: 23 Sept. 2012

Description: UFO

Disposition: Identified

Findings: Lens Flare

Synopsis: On 23 Sept. 2012, at sunrise, the witness was taking photos of the sky with a camera. While reviewing the photos, the witness noticed a strange object on the right end of one photo. The witness submitted the photo to API for analysis.

Evidence Submitted: A photo of a UFO.

Initial Action: The team opened this UFO investigation by treating the phenomenon as an AN1: an anomaly that left temporary physical effects, such as lights in the sky and similar phenomena. The team's preliminary analysis of the video indicated the UFO was, more than likely, a catadioptric lens flare.

Investigation and Findings: The witness claimed that he did not personally observe the UFO while taking photos of the sunset, which the team recognized as a common indicator of a lens flare. The witness, in fact, noticed the UFO later that day while reviewing the photos. Additionally, the investigators noticed the sun was also within the picture's frame of view, indicating the likely source of the lens flare. In an effort to positively identify the object as a lens flare, the investigators obtained the original photo and applied standard cross-section analysis to it. Their analysis of the photo indicated that the anomaly intersected with the known light source (the sun) inside the frame of view on the photo's left side, creating a lens flare.

Object Details: Lens flares are created when non-image-forming light enters the camera lens and subsequently hit the camera's film or digital sensor.[23] A lens flare often appears as a polygonal shape, giving the appearance of a "flying disk or saucer."

CASE: 12-013-AN4

Location: Washington, D.C.

Date of Event: 19 July 2012

Description: Alien Signal

Disposition: Identified

Findings: Pareidolia

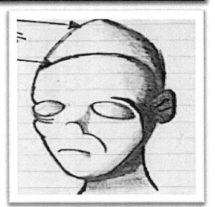

Synopsis: The witness to this sighting submitted several documents alleging contact with extraterrestrials. According to the witness, the extraterrestrials transmitted a signal containing 3D images at a high rate of speed and at a minimum of at least two frames per second. The witness analyzed the alleged signal and concluded that the transmission was comprised of several animations layered upon each other. Each layer had a varying degree of detail and provided information regarding biological forms, architectural designs, and environments. According to the witness, the "Targzissians," a species of extraterrestrial origin, transmitted the signal.

Evidence Submitted: A sketch of the alien entity, still images from the signal, and an executive summary written by the witness.

Initial Action: The team opened this UFO case by treating the phenomenon as an AN4: an interaction of a witness with occupants or entities. The team performed initial indices checks on the witness, which indicated a hoax.

Investigation and Findings: The investigators conducted open-source checks and learned that the witness had submitted the report of the alleged alien signal to multiple UFO organizations and the U.S. government. The witness complained that most of the organizations did not respond, while those that did replied that the witness was experiencing pareidolia and hysteria. The team's investigative research also indicated that the witness was associated with multiple conspiracy groups; he often alleged that a Targzissian invasion was imminent. After attending several interviews, the witness failed to cooperate further with the investigation and stopped all communications with the team. The team eventually closed the case, classifying it as "pareidolia and conspiracy claims."

Object Details: Pareidolia.

CASE: 12-074-AN1

Location: Pell City, AL

Date of Event: 01 Oct. 2012

Description: UFO

Disposition: Identified

Findings: Lens Flare

Synopsis: On the morning of 1 Oct. 2012, the witness to this sighting used a mobile phone to take a photo of the sunrise. While reviewing the photo, the witness noticed a strange object in it. The witness provided the photo to API for analysis.

Evidence Submitted: A photo of the UFO.

Initial Action: The team opened this UFO investigation by treating the phenomenon as an AN1: an anomaly that left temporary physical effects, such as lights in the sky and similar phenomena. The team's preliminary analysis of the video indicated the UFO was, more than likely, a catadioptric lens flare.

Investigation and Findings: After an interview with the witness, the investigators learned that the witness did not personally observe the UFO. The investigators applied cross-line analysis on the photo, which indicated the UFO was a lens flare. The sun, which was also in the frame of view, was the source of the lens flare.

Object Details: Lens flares are created when non-image-forming light enters the camera lens and subsequently hit the camera's film or digital sensor.[24] The lens flare often appears as a polygonal shape, giving the appearance of a "flying disk or saucer."

CASE: 12-077-CE1

Location: Newcastle, U.K.

Date of Event: Mid-2008

Description: Man in Black

Disposition: Identified

Findings: Paranoia

Synopsis: The witness to this sighting claimed that while taking a walk to his home, he was approached by a very tall "MIB." According to the witness, the Man in Black was wearing all black and had a very pale face; his entire eyes were black, and he wore strange buttons on his coat. The Man in Black spoke softly. He asked about the witness's family and asked if he could talk to the witness's twin brother. The witness told the Man in Black he had no twin brother, and the witness left. A few days later, the witness saw the same Man in Black wandering around the witness's work location.

Evidence Submitted: A photo of the Man in Black.

Initial Action: The team opened this UFO case by treating the phenomenon as an AN4: an interaction of a witness with occupants or entities. The team performed initial indices checks on the witness, which indicated a hoax.

Investigation and Findings: After conducting several e-mail conversations and interviews with the witness, the investigators learned that the alleged sighting of the Man in Black was nothing more then a case of mistaken identity. At the time of the encounter, the witness believed the strange man's behavior was "spooky" and that the clothing the Man in Black was wearing was unusual. However, after reflecting upon the incident later, the witness came to believe the man was just "a weirdo" and, more than likely, was not associated with extraterrestrials or UFO phenomena.

Object Details: Mistaken identity and paranoia.

CASE: 12-075-AN1

Location: Morley, U.K.

Date of Event: 29 Sept. 2012

Description: UFO

Disposition: Identified

Findings: Meteor

Synopsis: On 29 Sept. 2012, at midnight, the witness to this sighting was sitting on a porch when she saw a very bright light in the sky. The light appeared to get brighter and then slowly faded away. The bright light lasted about ten seconds.

Evidence Submitted: A sketch of the UFO.

Initial Action: The team opened this UFO investigation by treating the phenomenon as an AN1: an anomaly that left temporary physical effects, such as lights in the sky and similar phenomena.

Investigation and Findings: The investigators interviewed the witness to this sighting on two separate occasions. According to the witness, the bright object appeared 45 degrees above the horizon and slowly dimmed until it fell away. After the interview, the investigators conducted research regarding any known meteor activity in the West Yorkshire area. According to several credible websites that track meteor reports, several witnesses reported a large meteor on the same date and time as the one at which the witness to this sighting saw the UFO. The investigators compared the description of the object provided by the witness and the descriptions of meteor activity in the same area, and they concluded the object was a meteor.

Object Details: Meteor.

CHAPTER THREE

THE ANALYSIS

When a truth is necessary, the reason for it can be found by analysis; that is, by resolving it into simpler ideas and truths until the primary ones are reached.

-- Gottfried Leibniz

THE ANALYSIS

The investigations API conducted were challenging. Many of the witnesses the team interviewed, for example, were considered respectable members of their communities; in some cases, the witnesses were trained observers, such as former military members, police officers, and pilots. In contrast, the team also found that a good number of the witnesses could not be deemed credible; on a few occasions, the witnesses provided misdirection and false testimony. Overall, the team determined that the physical evidence provided by all of the witnesses—and, for that matter, the evidence collected at sites reported to have had alleged extraterrestrial activity—was lackluster at best.

By adhering to the API investigative process, the team succeeded in the following actions:

- Spending over 2,000 hours collecting data from witnesses.
- Consulting with experts from a wide range of scientific disciplines.
- Researching UFO-related archives.
- Conducting site visits to locations of alleged extraterrestrial activity.

After the team completed UFO investigations, its members fused the data, providing the team and the UFO community with an analytical assessment of the phenomena. Please note that the analytical assessment provided in this chapter is the result of data exclusively collected during API investigations, not gathered from other UFO organizations' reports conducted outside of API's Case Management System.

API's investigative process established that most UFO sightings were misidentified terrestrial objects, natural phenomena, hoaxes, or outbreaks of hysteria. Our investigations revealed most UFOs were misidentified as one of the following:

- Satellites in LEO
- High-altitude flying aircraft
- Airships or high-altitude balloons
- Lens flares or dirty camera optics
- Abnormal cloud formations
- Insects
- Celestial objects
- Defense industry tests of weapon systems
- Hoaxes (witting and/or unwitting)
- Pareidolia and/or hysteria

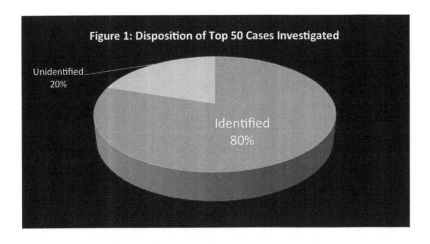

Of the UFO investigations completed by API, 80% were resolved as identified, while the remaining 20% were either unresolved or closed as "unidentified" (Figure 1). Of the fifty cases completed and described in this book, causes for the phenomena included the following: 32% were man-made objects, 30% were natural phenomena, 8% were hoaxes, 10% were pareidolia; the remaining 20% were closed as "unidentified" (Figure 2). Of the 80% of the investigations resolved, 40% were caused by man-made objects, 37% were caused by natural phenomena, 10% were classified as hoaxes, and 13% were either caused by pareidolia or hysteria (Figure 3).

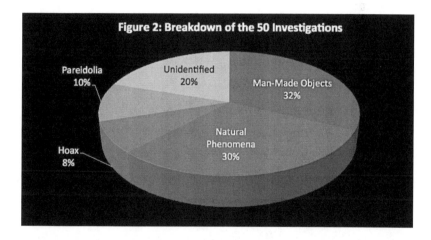

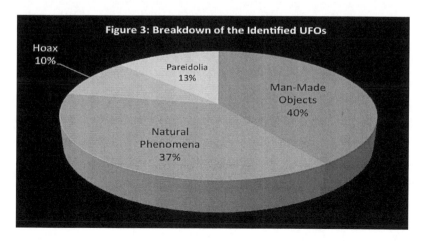

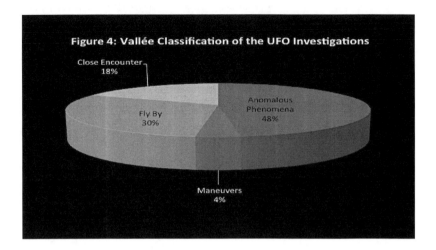

Furthermore, as per the Vallée classification, API classified its UFO investigations as follows: 48% anomalous phenomena, 30% fly-bys, 18% close encounters, and 4% maneuvers (Figure 4).

Lastly, it is essential to emphasize that the cases API closed as "identified" were marked as such because of the following:

- The witness provided a detailed description of the sighting.
- The witness cooperated with the investigators.
- The witness provided a photo, video and/or a sketch.
- The UFO sighting occurred within the last five years.

Checking cases against these four conditions allowed API investigators to fully exploit the investigative process and identify each object in a timely manner.

In contrast, API closed most of the unresolved cases as "unidentified" due to lack of witness cooperation or the event having taken place over five years prior to the investigation. Of the ten unidentified cases, only 40% of the witnesses cooperated with the investigators (Figure 4). The other 60% of the witnesses, however, presented at least one of the following problems:

- They could not provide enough data because the UFO sightings occurred too long ago.
- They did not cooperate with the investigators during the investigation.

Although these ten cases were closed as "unidentified," any hypothesis suggesting the cases were in fact based on extraterrestrial origins would be far-reaching.

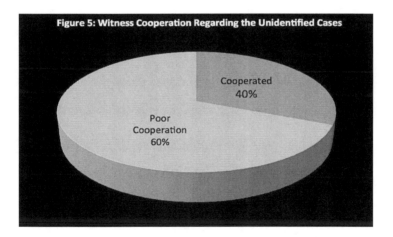

CHAPTER FOUR

REVIVING UFOLOGY

You can tell when something is not moving forward anymore: when the doubts you have about it don't go away.

-- Jeffrey Eugenides

MOVING FORWARD

In the last year, I have identified an array of noteworthy concerns that I believe have derailed the study of Ufology. Regrettably, these problems have ruined the subject, degrading it to a point at which any discussion regarding UFOs is no longer taken seriously by society:

- There is a lack of investigative data-sharing among UFO groups and investigators.
- Most UFO conferences are a joke.
- The Internet has become a focal point at which people create, store, and disseminate thousands of fake UFO photos and videos, conspiracy theories, and hoaxes.

First, the scope of the problem regarding Ufology is not so much trying to find proof, beyond a reasonable doubt, that extraterrestrials exist. Instead, the primary problem crippling Ufology today is that there is no cohesive cooperation among the cadre of UFO groups out there, each claiming to be better than the other. Most, if not all, of the UFO research and investigations groups I have encountered compartmentalize their UFO reports; in almost all cases, they never make public the results of their investigations, thus keeping other UFO investigators from analyzing the reports. For example, while API conducted its UFO investigations, the team found cooperation with other UFO groups was lackluster at best. In most cases, any request for information that might have shaped or moved forward an API investigation were simply ignored by these organizations.

In my opinion, the newer UFO groups, which are slowly evolving, are a threat to established UFO groups. Rather than embracing the newer generation, made up of people who are savvy in the use of emerging technologies, the established UFO groups appear to isolate themselves, which wrecks their credibility. On one occasion, I was offered a leadership position in another UFO group, but the offer was conditional: I would have had to dismantle API. I rejected the offer because I knew API was making a noticeable impact in Ufology. Therefore, I stress that if the UFO community wishes to revive Ufology and bring it back to the worthy subject it once was, this data-sharing issue must be resolved immediately, and cooperation among investigators must solidify.

Second, in the last few decades, UFO conventions and expos have become gathering points at which conspiracy theorists, crypto-zoologists, and pseudo-psychics come together and share information that has no purpose in a Ufology setting. For example, many of the UFO conferences I have attended have been inundated with topics related to Bigfoot, the Loch Ness Monster, chupacabra, Mothman, and even inter-dimensional beings (which contactees claim to have been in direct contact with). At a recent local UFO conference, I observed the following inappropriate events:

- A vendor attempted to persuade attendees to purchase massage therapy using "magic rocks and crystals." According to the vendor, the origin of the rocks and crystals was unknown, but he stressed they harnessed an

"inter-dimensional power" that could heal people... only, however, if you purchased a therapy session with him.
- A group of "mind-control psychics" claimed they were in direct contact with inter-dimensional beings. These psychics claimed they could tell people what the inter-dimensional beings were talking about at that very moment—for a price, of course.

At many of these UFO conferences, the main topic continued to center on decades-old events, such as the following:

- The Kenneth Arnold Sighting of 1947,
- the Roswell UFO Incident of 1947,
- and the alleged abduction of Betty and Barney Hill in 1961.

It is beyond my comprehension why these topics continue to choke UFO conferences, given that in the last 70 years hundreds of other worthy UFO incidents have occurred. To salvage these UFO conferences, and more importantly, to attract the newer and younger generation to them, UFO conference organizers must remove the topics that have no business in a UFO setting. Therefore, as we enter the twenty-first century, older UFO incidents must be shelved and more recent UFO news must be expanded upon.

Lastly, modern computer technology has become the chief culprit in creating and disseminating thousands of fake UFO photos and videos. The Internet has become the largest depository of these fake photos and videos. When we couple these two factors together, it becomes obvious that investigators can no longer accept any digital evidence without an extraordinary degree of skepticism. Even worse, the thousands of so-called UFO websites and depositories of alleged UFO photos have attracted an army of arm-chair UFO investigators—many of them come to their own investigative conclusions without even conducting witness interviews or fieldwork. On many UFO and conspiracy websites, skeptics and believers spend more time debating each other than they do in coming together to solve UFO phenomena.

Unfortunately, the lack of data-sharing among UFO groups, cheesy UFO conventions, and swarms of Internet hoaxers and conspiracy theorists have all converged. This convergence has forced most, if not all, literature regarding Ufology to be shelved at the occult section of local bookstores or libraries. Ufology, in short, has been derailed to the point at which science, the U.S. government, and the general public no longer take the topic seriously.

The first step in reviving Ufology for the twenty-first century, in my opinion, must come from within UFO groups. Leaders in the UFO community must be willing to break away from the tradition of compartmentalizing their UFO investigations so that other investigators can incorporate the data into their own investigations. In the process known as "data fusion," UFO investigators should be allowed to collect, gather, and analyze as much UFO investigative data as they need. This process will allow each UFO investigator to develop a strategic analytical picture of the phenomena, rather than being held hostage to only researching UFO activity in his or her immediate geographic area.

Second, in a step that is just as important as the first, leaders in the UFO community must refrain from allowing their UFO conventions to be high-jacked by vendors, speakers, and topics that have no purpose in a UFO convention. Bigfoot, the Loch Ness Monster, and the paranormal, for example, should not be allowed at any UFO convention. Additionally, these UFO conventions should be centered on current and fact-based presentations, not topics that entertain the physics of interstellar travel; inter-dimensional beings; alleged top-secret, anti-gravity propulsion systems; or conspiracy theories regarding alleged U.S. government efforts to reverse-engineer extraterrestrial technology. These topics belong at a science-fiction convention, not at a UFO convention.

Finally, the serious UFO investigator must limit his or her Internet research to credible sources of information and refrain from conducting too much research on conspiracy websites or UFO blogs that lack credibility. The UFO investigator must be willing to set aside the extraterrestrial hypotheses and collect data from a nuts-and-bolts perspective. Much of this investigative data can be derived from the following:

- witnesses;
- experts and sources from a variety of scientific, U.S. government, and defense industry fields;
- *in situ* research and data collection where the activity is occurring;
- and data from other credible UFO investigations.

In closing, a convergence of three significant problems has derailed Ufology: a lack of data sharing, cheesy UFO conferences, and the littering of the Internet with hoaxes and conspiracies. There are, in contrast, several opportunities slowly emerging on the horizon that could salvage Ufology. First, the older generation of established Ufologists are slowly fading away, making room for a younger, more advanced generation of investigators capable of reshaping the Ufology landscape. Second, on the other end of the Internet spectrum, innovative UFO groups like API are exploiting the Internet and social media in order to educate the public regarding UFOs and, more importantly, what are not UFOs. These cyberspace efforts are centered on ensuring future UFO conferences, expos, and forums are not high-jacked by topics that have no bearing on Ufology. As these opportunities slowly converge, I have no doubt the twenty-first century will witness the revival of Ufology.

API Photo: Antonio Paris, the Director of API, attends a variety of UFO conferences to educate the public regarding UFOs.

GLOSSARY

Alpha Centauri: Alpha Centauri is the brightest star in the southern constellation of Centaurus. Although it appears to the unaided eye as a single object, Alpha Centauri is actually a binary star system.

Altocumulus Castellanus Formations: Clouds named for their tower-like projections, which billow upwards from the base of each cloud. The base of the cloud can form as low as 2,000 meters (6,500 feet) or as high as 6,000 meters (20,000 feet).

Apogee: The point in the orbit of an object orbiting the earth at the greatest distance from the center of the earth.

Counterintelligence: Efforts made by intelligence organizations to prevent hostile or enemy intelligence organizations from successfully gathering and collecting intelligence.

Counterintelligence Field Activity (CIFA): A former United States Department of Defense agency whose size and budget were classified. CIFA was created by a directive from the Secretary of Defense (Number 5105.67) on February 19, 2002, and shut down on August 8, 2008.

Cumulus Humilis: A low- to middle-range cloud that is commonly referred to as "fair weather cumulus." In hot countries and over mountainous terrain these clouds occur at up to 6,000 meters (20,000 feet) altitude, though elsewhere they are typically found at lower altitudes.

Electronic Intelligence (ELINT): Intelligence derived from electromagnetic radiations from foreign sources (other than radioactive sources).

Electronic Voice Phenomena (EVP): In the paranormal industry, this term refers to purported electronically generated noises that resemble speech but are supposedly not the result of intentional voice recordings or renderings.

Exchangeable Image File Format (EXIF): A standard that specifies the formats for images, sound, and ancillary tags used by digital cameras (including smartphones), scanners, and other systems handling image and sound files recorded by digital cameras.

Extraterrestrial: This term may refer to any object or being beyond (*extra-*) Earth (*terrestrial*). It is derived from the Latin Root *extra* ("outside," "outwards") and *terrestris* ("earthly").

Investigative Process: Actions and steps taken during an investigation that result in delivering a final report that conveys the investigation results.

Lens Flares: The light scattered in lens systems through generally unwanted image formation mechanisms, such as internal reflection or scattering from material inhomogeneities in the lens.

Low Earth Orbit (LEO): An orbit below an altitude of 2,000 kilometers (1,200 miles).

Men in Black (MIB): In American popular culture and in UFO conspiracy theories, "MIB" are men dressed in black suits who claim to be government agents and who harass or threaten UFO witnesses to keep the latter quiet about what they (the witnesses) have seen. It is sometimes implied that the MIB may be extraterrestrials themselves.

National Aeronautics and Space Administration (NASA): The agency of the U.S. government responsible for the nation's civilian space program and for aeronautics and aerospace research.

National Security Agency (NSA): The NSA is a cryptologic intelligence agency of the U.S. Department of Defense responsible for the collection and analysis of foreign communications and foreign signals intelligence, as well as for protecting U.S. government communications and information systems.

Pareidolia: A psychological phenomenon involving a vague and random stimulus (often an image or sound) being perceived as significant. A few common examples include seeing images of animals or faces in clouds, seeing the man in the moon, and hearing hidden messages on records when they are played in reverse.

Perigee: The point in the orbit of an object orbiting the earth nearest to the center of the earth.

Project Blue Book: This term refers to studies of unidentified flying objects (UFOs) conducted by the U.S. Air Force. Started in 1952, this was the third revival of such a study (the first two of its kind being Projects Sign and Grudge). A termination order from the U.S. Air Force was given for the study in December 1969, and all activity under its auspices ceased in January 1970.

Rayleigh Scattering: The elastic scattering of light or other electromagnetic radiation by particles much smaller than the wavelength of the light. The particles may be individual atoms or molecules. This scattering can occur when light travels through transparent solids and liquids, although it is most prominently seen in gases.

The Federal Aviation Administration (FAA): An agency of the U.S. Department of Transportation that has authority to regulate and oversee all aspects of civil aviation in the U.S.

The Mutual UFO Network (MUFON): An American non-profit organization that investigates cases of reported UFO sightings. It is one of the oldest and largest UFO-investigative organizations in the U.S.

The National UFO Reporting Center (NUFORC): An organization in the U.S. that investigates UFO sightings and/or extraterrestrial contacts. NUFORC has been in continuous operation since 1974.

The SETI Institute (SETI): The SETI Institute is a not-for-profit organization whose mission is to "explore, understand, and explain the origin, nature, and prevalence of life in the universe."

Tactics, Techniques, and Procedures (TTP): The doctrine an organization applies to adjust its products, organizations, and processes to maximize the support provided to the customer.

United Kingdom Royal Entomology Society: The Royal Entomological Society plays a major national and international role in disseminating information about insects and improving communication between entomologists. The Society was founded in 1833 as the

Entomological Society of London and is the successor to a number of short-lived societies dating back to 1745.

Unidentified Flying Object (UFO): An unusual, apparent anomaly in the sky that is not readily identifiable to the observer as any known object; it is often associated with extraterrestrial life.

Unmanned Aerial Vehicle (UAV): Commonly known as a drone, this is an aircraft without a human pilot on board. Either computers in the vehicle control its flight autonomously, or it is under the remote control of a navigator or pilot.

Vega: The brightest star in the constellation Lyra, Vega is the fifth-brightest star in the night sky and the second-brightest star in the northern celestial hemisphere. It is a relatively close star at only twenty-five light-years from Earth.

Waxing Gibbous: The phase of the moon at which more than half the circle is visible; it occurs just before the full moon, when the entire orb is visible.

REFERENCES USED
(ENDNOTES)

1. Sagan, Carl and Thornton Page. "Definition of a UFO" UFOs: A Scientific Debate. 1995
2. United States Air Force. Project Blue Book. http://www.af.mil/information/factsheets/factsheet.asp?id=188
3. Department of Defense. http://www.defense.gov/releases/release.aspx?releaseid=12106
4. Vallée, Jacques F. "Physical Analyses in Ten Cases of Unexplained Aerial Objects with Material Samples." Journal of Scientific Exploration, 12.3 [1998]: 360–361.
5. The National Aeronautics and Space Administration. "Cosmos 1953 Satellite Data." National Space Science Data Center Master Catalog. http://nssdc.gsfc.nasa.gov/nmc/spacecraftDisplay.do?id=1988-050A
6. "Vega is the Harp Star." Earth and Sky. http://earthsky.org/brightest-stars/vega-brilliant-blue-white-is-third-brightest-star
7. Cambridge in Colour. "Understanding Camera Lens Flares." http://www.cambridgeincolour.com/tutorials/lens-flare.htm
8. Carroll, Robert Todd. "A Collection of Strange Beliefs, Amusing Deceptions, and Dangerous Delusions." John Wiley & Sons: 2003. Retrieved 6 April 2010.

9. SINA Technology News. "China's Outstanding UFO Investigation: Fly Rod Haunted World (Part Two)."
10. Clouds Online. "The Cumulus Cloud." http://www.clouds-online.com/cloud_atlas/cumulus/cumulus.htm
11. The National Aeronautics and Space Administration. "Cosmos 1733 Satellite Data." National Space Science Data Center Master Catalog. http://nssdc.gsfc.nasa.gov/nmc/masterCatalog.do?sc=1986-018A
12. Heath, Sir Thomas Little. (1981). A History of Greek Mathematics, Volume II: From Aristarchus to Diophantus.
13. Advance Camera, Inc. "Dirty Camera Sensors." http://www.advancecamera.com/2012/02/17/dirty-dslr-camera-sensor/
14. UFO Grid. "Men in Black." http://ufogrid.com/ufo/articles/real-men-black
15. World Surveillance Group, Inc. Argus One Airship. http://www.wsgi.com/argus.php
16. The National Aeronautics and Space Administration. "Iridium 44 Satellite Data." National Space Science Data Center Master Catalog. http://nssdc.gsfc.nasa.gov/nmc/spacecraftOrbit.do?id=1997-077B
17. "Understanding Purple Fringing." Digital Photography Review. http://www.dpreview.com
18. Cambridge in Colour. Understanding Camera Lens Flares. http://www.cambridgeincolour.com/tutorials/lens-flare.htm
19. Bohren, C. F. and D. Huffman. "Rayleigh Scattering." Absorption and Scattering of Light by Small Particles. New York: John Wiley, 1983.

20. Northrup Grumman, http://www.as.northropgrumman.com
21. Box Office Mojo. "Box Office Mojo: The Fourth Kind." Retrieved 2010-09-12.
22. The National Aeronautics and Space Administration. "Iridium 44 Satellite Data." National Space Science Data Center Master Catalog. http://nssdc.gsfc.nasa.gov/nmc/masterCatalog.do?sc=2002-005E
23. Cambridge in Colour. "Understanding Camera Lens Flares." http://www.cambridgeincolour.com/tutorials/lens-flare.htm
24. Cambridge in Colour. "Understanding Camera Lens Flares." http://www.cambridgeincolour.com/tutorials/lens-flare.ht

NOTES